Mary
The Blessed Virgin of Islam

MARY

عليها السلام

THE BLESSED VIRGIN OF ISLAM

Aliah Schleifer

Foreword by T.J. Winter

FONS VITAE

Third Edition 2008

Printed in Canada

Library of Congress Catalog Card Number: 98-71660

ISBN-1-887752-02-1

This edition published by
Fons Vitae
(Gray Henry, Director)
49 Mockingbird Valley Drive
Louisville, KY 40207-1366
email: Grayh@aol.com
website: www.fonsvitae.com

IN MEMORIAM

IN LATE 1997, my Cairo friend of two decades, Aliah Schleifer died quickly and unexpectedly in New York surrounded by her parents, family and a few close friends. As her physical being diminished, she became translucent and her spirit shone through. She had never appeared so radiant or so beautiful. Her pious life had been an example to many, and her courage and strength in death, inspiring. She asked me to publish her doctoral dissertation, recently completed at Exeter, England. There can be no doubt that the qualities exemplified in the life and essence of the Virgin Mary (عليها السلام), to which Aliah devoted her last years, must have been both sustaining and a great comfort as her life drew to completion.

As the form of this dissertation would not have lent itself to be fully appreciated by a general readership, I personally took the liberty of making certain changes and of including short biographies of the scholars upon whose works Aliah drew.

In a world wrought by the kinds of crippling stereotypes which hinder peace, particularly among religious faiths, it seemed to me that this work on Mary could be not only of help in the Christian-Muslim dialogue, but an inspiration to women in general. It never had occurred to me that a woman might have been considered to be among the prophets sent to mankind.

Very few Christians have any idea of the importance of the Virgin Mary in Islam, and that Islamic doctrine maintains that Jesus (عليه السلام) and Mary are the only two in all eternity to have been born without sin and that Mary is considered the purest woman in all creation. She is considered to be an example for both men and women.

Aliah was pleased that I was going to bring out *Mary the Blessed Virgin of Islam* as a sequel to her master's thesis, *Motherhood in Islam*, which is valuable for the understanding of family integrity in the Islamic social structure, as well as very reassuring to women in that motherhood has such great rewards.

I cannot express with sufficiency my gratitude to Timothy Winter of Cambridge University and to Patricia Salazar for their invaluable efforts and contributions, without which this small volume would not have come to be. And may I be forgiven for the imperfections for which I am responsible.

Gray Henry
Fons Vitae

Contents

In Memoriam 5
Foreword 9
Introduction 15
Acknowledgements 17
Key Persons Mentioned in the Text 18

1 Life of Mary 21
2 The Mother 45
3 The Symbol of Submission, the Devout, the Faithful 55
4 The Pure, the Best of Women 62
5 The Sincere, the Righteous: Saint or Prophetess 73
6 Conclusion 95

Appendix: Pictures in the Kaʿba 101
Notes 106
Bibliography 139
Annotated Index 150

PUBLISHER'S NOTE: The conventions of British spelling, punctuation, and hyphenation have been maintained throughout this edition.

The reader also will notice that following the mention of the name of a prophet in the text, there is a small seal in Arabic. Around the globe, be it in China or Nigeria, no Muslim would refer to the Prophet Muḥammad (ﷺ), to Jesus (عليه السلام) or to Mary (عليها السلام), or to any of the other prophets, such as David or Zachariah (عليهم السلام), without adding: "May God's peace be upon him, her, or them."

FOREWORD

IN HIS WONDERFULLY anecdotal *Book of Travels*, the seventeenth-century Turkish voyager Evliya Chelebi recalls an incident which he once witnessed in the Süleymaniye mosque in Istanbul. A group of European Catholic tourists, setting foot for the first time inside the incomparable structure, were so awe-struck that they stood, rooted to the spot. They then tossed their hats in the air, and uttered the exultant cry, *Maria*!

Chelebi, as a believing Muslim, was not scandalised to hear this exclamation in a mosque. He would have been taught from early childhood that Islam accords an honoured place to Mary (عليها السلام), the virginal mother of Jesus (عليه السلام) the Messiah. In fact, the Qur'ān has somewhat more to say about her than has the Bible, and credits her with an active and even prophetic role which has intrigued modern readers concerned with issues of gender. Such an overlap between two worlds of belief deserves careful scrutiny, which is why the present book, whose intention is to make available an analytic anthology of Muslim remarks on the Virgin, is to be warmly welcomed.

Dr. Schleifer's is not the first work to deal with Islam's distinctive Mariology. Monographs by Abd el-Jalil (1950) and V. Courtois (1954) made a good beginning, albeit from a pre-conciliar Catholic viewpoint which sometimes appeared to define Islam as a kind of Christianity *manqué*; while more recently, Geoffrey Parrinder (1965), Roger Arnaldez (1980), and Jane McAuliffe (1991) have included more appreciative accounts of the Qur'ānic Mary in their biographies of the Muslim Jesus. No less instructive are two Muslim devotional works, both published in 1991: *La Fille d'Imran* by Patrick Pahlavi, nephew of the last Shah of Iran, and

Sheikh Muzaffer Ozak's *Blessed Virgin Mary*, translated from Turkish by the able hand of Muhtar Holland. Dr. Schleifer has now bridged the gap between the several approaches by writing as a Muslim who is also committed to a Western academic method.

Although interfaith communication was not the author's primary purpose, Muslim and Christian readers engaged in dialogue will find much of immediate value in this book, written as it was by a committed muslima for whom Mary was of real personal importance, and who was deeply concerned by what she saw as the deterioration of her religion's image among many Western Christians. 'Man is an enemy to what he does not understand,' the caliph ʿAlī is said to have remarked; and Dr. Schleifer saw it as a painful irony that Islam, which is closer to Christianity than any other faith, should for Western minds have often appeared as the quintessence of everything that is foreign and unintelligible.

Mary, hallowed differently on opposite coasts of the Mediterranean, offers a revelatory sign of this tension. Family feuds can sometimes be more bitter than wars fought between strangers; yet family members can also, with goodwill, achieve a unique closeness. For most of our shared history, Christianity has not understood Islam's Mariology at all; while Islam has grasped the Mariologies of Christianity only imperfectly. Are the irreducible dissonances that must remain still large enough to obstruct a true sense of ease and conviviality with the 'Other', or does scholarship offer a final emancipation from a centuries-long mutual alienation?

The Mary that Dr. Schleifer reveals is both familiar and strange to Christian readers. Her immaculacy remains, but bears a different weight amid Islam's robust affirmations of the human body. She is mother to Jesus the Messiah, but Islam's Christ often seems more recognisable to the revisionist New Testament scholarship which denies that Jesus claimed divinity for himself, than to the teaching of the Church as this has been preserved down the centuries from Nicaea and Chalcedon.

For most Christians, Mary is the Mother of God, yet for Muslims, although she is a perfected saint and a focus of intercessory hopes, she exercises no indispensable role in the economy of salvation. For while Islam and Christianity concur in affirming a perfect Creator God, they differ, as their rival Marys show, on how that God touches individual souls and brings them to perfection.

Christians discern liberation in a God who descended into history out of infinite love, and gave himself to ransom us from sin. Muslims, whose narrative of the Fall excludes any understanding of original sin, must respectfully dissent from this view. The divine love, duly conjoined with justice, ensures that a full and liberative forgiveness is available to all who freely turn to God in penitence, in the way that has been so amply witnessed by great saints today and in the Muslim past. For Muslims, the Blessed Virgin is not *theotokos,* the woman that bore God Himself and gazed in love upon Him as He lay in straw. Instead she bears witness to the presence of the God who need not 'come' into the world, because He has never been 'absent' from it. The Qur'ān has said that He is nearer to us than the jugular vein, or, as a saint of Alexandria expressed it, 'only God's extreme nearness to you is what veils you from Him.' The very name of the Qur'ān, which is the Muslim 'Word', itself signifies a 'Reading': it urges us to comprehend the world as a text built out of signs, as a universal theophany which is not fallen, but is merely unread. Hence what Schopenhauer called the 'optimism' of Islam. Atonement, expiation and redemption can never be resonant terms in the Muslim lexicon.

Dr. Schleifer reminds us of a further distinction between the Mariologies of Islam and its great predecessor. For Christians, Mary is unrivalled as the model of female perfection. Islam, however, has debated the merits of several women. A ḥadīth which has come down to us in more than one version suggests that there have been four 'Perfect Women' in history. One is Āsiya, the wife of the Pharoah who challenged Moses (عليه السلام), revered by the Muslim chroniclers as a saint who endured the rages of her husband. A ḥadīth tells us that a woman who suffers maltreatment from her husband will be rewarded as was Āsiya; and she hence becomes a model and a source of hope for women caught abusive relationships. Another 'Perfect Woman' is Khadīja, the first to believe in the message of the Prophet (ﷺ), and who, as a successful businesswoman who took the Prophet into her employ, provides a traditional model for Muslim women who have sought a living in the world. Thirdly, there is Mary. And fourthly, there is the Prophet's daughter Fāṭima.

Devout Muslims have for centuries debated which of these four is to receive the highest glory in heaven. Mary and Fāṭima often seem to be placed equally. Traditional Islamic sources sometimes present Fāṭima as a latter-day reminiscence of the Virgin, receiving her title of *al-batūl:* as for instance when after miraculously providing food for the hungry, she quotes Mary's 'This is from God's presence; truly God provides for whomsoever He will without any reckoning.'

But although Mary is a spiritual inspiration, it is Fāṭima who has more usually supplied the role model for Muslim women in their search for practical perfection. Mary's virginity is revered as her greatest miracle, but Islam's positive view of sexuality, and the value Muslim piety has traditionally attached to the married state as the preferred matrix for spiritual life, have rendered a true *imitatio mariae* impossible. Fāṭima's spiritual exaltation, proclaimed by the Prophet himself, far from appearing compromised by her biological fulfilment, was sustained and vindicated by it. She is, in the Muslim memory, the fountainhead of the Prophet's revered descendents, the ancestress of saints, the mother of tragic heroes. Through her non-virginal but no less immaculate example, Muslim women have found their assurance that the approach to God can be enhanced rather than impeded by the normal functions of womanhood.

So: what hope for future understanding through the person of Mary, or Maryam as Muslims know her? It is within a theologically coherent framework which upholds the objective status of one's own interpretation of revelation that the person of Maryam can best serve us in dialogue. She should remind us that true respect and fellowship between religions can only be grounded in the mature acknowledgement of what is irreconcilable, although we can and must also proclaim and celebrate what we hold in common. The alternate readings of her do not diminish her shared significance as a Jewish woman who has reminded Christians and Muslims of a host of fundamental truths. The spiritual gifts of women, the sanctity of Jerusalem, the ascetic holiness of Jesus, the efficacy of prayer and the value of trust: these are only a few of the shared lessons that prove how surely Mary can function as a unifying symbol.

It is often remarked that the religions can no longer afford the luxury of mutual rivalry, and that it is in the interests of them all to acknowledge that each now faces only one significant enemy, namely the spirit of negation and relativism which defines the modern world. Such a perspective holds that confronted with the triumph of sophisticated egotism the religions must nurture a style of cooperation which respects their differences while permitting a shared counter-attack against the spirit of modernity and now postmodernity, which by denying the unique Source of the Word has made an idol of everything in existence.

Hopeful foretokens of such a common front are not lacking. The 1994 United Nations Population Conference in Cairo witnessed amicable and often fruitful efforts of cooperation between Muslim and Vatican delegates. On a smaller scale, in England, contact between Muslims and Catholics has been flourishing. Let us begin Dr. Schleifer's book by recalling just one example of this heartening growth in trust. In 1991, a group of Muslims received permission to create a mosque from the former Priory of St. Anne, sited in a North London district whose Catholic population had largely moved away. After some debate, they elected to leave in place the inscription over the main entrance, taking it as a source of hope and as a reminder that, for believers, the fate of the world is not in our hands: *Sancta Maria, mater dolorosa, ora pro nobis.*

T. J. Winter
Faculty of Divinity
University of Cambridge

INTRODUCTION

ALIAH SCHLEIFER'S BOOK *Mary* (🌺) *The Blessed Virgin of Islam* is a unique work. It illustrates the revered position that the Virgin Mary (🌺) holds in the thought of Sunni Islam, as well as the respect and veneration with which ordinary Muslims regard her. The subject of the Virgin Mary is discussed comprehensively, from the perspective of the traditional scholars, using precise and clearly defined academic methodology.

An essential part of Islam is the acceptance of previous religions: 'Say: We believe in Allah, in what He revealed to Abraham, to Ishmael, to Isaac, to Jacob, and to the tribes, and in what Moses and Jesus received, and in what the prophets received from their Lord. We do not diferentiate between them, and we submit unto them. If they believe, then they are rightly guided. But if they turn away, then they are in schism, but Allah will suffice thee (for defence) against them, and He is the Hearer, the Omniscient'. (Qur'ān 2:136–37)

The Messiah and his early followers are praised in Islam, and are regarded among the elite of the pious. Jesus (عليه السلام) is counted among the prophets who hold rank of *ūlū al-ʿazm*, or 'the steadfast'. This is the greatest rank in Islam held only by five prophets: Noah, Abraham, Moses, Jesus and Mohammad (ﷺ). According to the Qur'ān, Jesus announced the coming of the Prophet Muḥammad, and therefore belief in Jesus is part of belief in Islam: 'Jesus the son of Mary said: O Children of Israel, I am the messenger of Allah unto you, confirming that which I possess of the Torah and bringing good tidings of a messenger who will come after me, whose name will be Aḥmad. And when he came to them with clear proofs, they said: This is obvious magic'. (Qur'ān 61:6)

Muslims also believe in the Second Coming of the Messiah: 'Verily he is the sign of the Hour. So do not doubt it and follow me. This is the Straight Path'. (Qur'ān 43:61) There are more than forty ḥadīths concerning the Second Coming of the Messiah The ḥadīths state that at the time of his Second Coming, all barriers between the believers will be removed, and they will become one community, seeking peace after war and stability after instabililty. As believers in this Second Coming of the Messiah, many Muslims see the importance of open discussion with the Christian community and anticipate that this sentiment would be reciprocal. Aliah Schleifer's present work corrects possible misunderstandings and provides a sound basis for such a dialogue.

This book is of great importance to the English-speaking world. It clarifies Islam's view of the Virgin Mary (🌺) through a discussion of the miracles and special blessings bestowed upon her according to the Qur'ān and traditional writings of Islam, and is therefore an appropriate stepping-stone for dialogue between all who love and revere her and her esteemed son.

Dr. ʿAlī Jumʿa Muḥammad
Professor of Islamic Law
Al-Azhar University

Acknowledgements

I WOULD LIKE to thank Dr. Ian R. Netton at Exeter University, for his guidance during the years of work required to complete the thesis on which this book is primarily based, and Prof. Antonio Vespertino Rodríguez (Oviedo University) for introducing me to some of the Spanish materials included in the Conclusion.

I would also like to state my appreciation for the cooperation of the staff of the following libraries and organizations: the library of the American University in Cairo; the British Museum Library; the University of Exeter Library; the Bodlian at Oxford University; the Instituto de Filología (Collección de Ribera y Asín), Madrid; the Biblioteca Nacional de Madrid; the Institut Dominicain d'Etudes Orientales, Cairo; and the Centre d'Études et de Recherches Ottomanes, Morisques, de Documentation et d'Information (CEROMDI), Tunis.

Finally, I would like to thank former professors, Dr. Aḥmed Ghunaym (AUC), Dr. El-Said M. Badawi (AUC), and Dr. Marsden Jones (formerly Prof. Emeritus, AUC) for encouraging me to embark on this project, Prof. S. A. Schleifer (AUC), Dr. Alan Godlas, Nur and Nureddin Durkee, Nihal ʿAbdRabbo, my colleagues, my parents and my children.

Aliah Schleifer

Key Persons Mentioned in the Text

BESIDES THE REFERENCES to the Virgin Mary found in the Qur'ān, the works of the following scholars and commentators have been drawn on in this book. Scholarly discussions on the Virgin Mary were carried on in regions stretching from Central Asia to Spain from the eighth century up to the present.

AḤMAD IBN ḤANBAL (d. 855). A great ḥadīth scholar of Baghdad, after whom the Ḥanbalī school of law is named.

BAYḌĀWĪ (d. 1293). A grammarian and theologian of Shiraz, whose commentary on the Qur'ān is noted for its thoroughness and clarity of exposition, particularly of grammatical and doctrinal points.

BUKHĀRĪ (d. 870). A great collector of ḥadīth, he lived in Central Asia. His ḥadīth anthology *al-Jāmiʿ al-Ṣaḥīḥ* is considered the most authoritative of all collections of ḥadīth.

ḌAḤḤĀK (d. 724). A ḥadīth scholar of Balkh in Central Asia who also gained a reputation as a Qur'ānic commentator.

DHAHABĪ (d. 1348). One of the best-known of all Arab historians, he spent most of his life in Damascus.

IBN ʿABBĀS (d. 687). A cousin of the Prophet, he is regarded as the greatest scholar among the first generation of Muslims, and as the founder of the science of Qur'ānic interpretation.

IBN ABI'L-DUNYĀ (d. 894). A storyteller and collector of ḥadīth, who taught several Abbasid princes in Baghdad.

IBN ʿASĀKIR (d. 1176). One of the best-known historians of Damascus, who also collected ḥadīth and wrote on the orthodox Ashʿarī school of theology.

IBN ḤAJAR (d. 1449). A major ḥadīth scholar of Cairo and Palestine, who authored the best-known commentary on the *Ṣaḥīḥ* of Bukhārī.

IBN ḤANBAL, see Aḥmad ibn Ḥanbal.

IBN HISHĀM (d. 828). The best-known biographer of the Prophet.

IBN ISḤĀQ (d. 767). A scholar of Madina and Baghdad, whose material formed the basis for the Prophetic biography of Ibn Hishām.

IBN JURAYJ (d. 767). A ḥadīth scholar of Mecca.

IBN KATHĪR (d. 1373). A well-known Qur'ānic commentator of Syria.

IBN SAʿD (d. 845). An Iraqi polymath remembered mainly for his great eight-volume encyclopedia of famous Muslims.

ʿIKRĪMA (d. 723). A manumitted slave of Ibn ʿAbbās who was one of the main transmitters of early intepretative material concerning the Qur'ān.

KAʿB AL-AḤBĀR (d.654). A Yemeni rabbi who converted to Islam and narrated a wealth of material.

MAQRĪZĪ (d. 1442). One of the most celebrated historians of medieval Egypt.

MUJĀHID (d. 722). A pupil of Ibn ʿAbbās, he was particularly concerned to identify the circumstances surrounding the revelation of each Qur'ānic verse.

MUQĀTIL (d. 767). A Central Asian scholar who compiled one of the earliest commentaries on the Qur'ān.

MUSLIM (d. 875). A Central Asian ḥadīth specialist, author of one of the most respected anthologies of ḥadīth.

NASĀ'Ī (d. 915). The author of one of the six best-known ḥadīth collections.

QATĀDA (d. 735). A pupil of the great Iraqi saint and scholar al-Ḥasan al-Baṣrī, he was a pioneer of Qur'ānic interpretation.

QURṬUBĪ (d. 1272). The greatest Spanish expert on Qur'ānic interpretation, author of one of the classic works of the genre.

QUSHAYRĪ (d. 1072). A leading orthodox scholar and Sufi of Central Asia, he wrote a spiritually-oriented commentary on the Qur'ān.

RĀZĪ (d. 1209). One of the greatest theologians of orthodox Islam, he was from Rayy in present-day Iran, and authored a massive intellectually-oriented commentary on the Holy Qur'ān.

RŪZBIHĀN AL-BAQLĪ (d. 1209). A Persian Sufi scholar, poet and author.

SUDDĪ (d. 744). An early Qur'ānic scholar from Kufa in Iraq.

SUYŪṬĪ (d. 1505). A medieval Egyptian polymath, author of almost a thousand books on all aspects of Islam.

ṬABARĀNĪ (d. 970). Central Asian author of several important collections of ḥadīth.

ṬABARĪ (d. 923). A Baghdad scholar whose encyclopedic knowledge of ḥadīth enabled him to write one of the most voluminous of all Qur'ānic commentaries.

TIRMIDHĪ (d. 892). The Central Asian compiler of an important early ḥadīth collection.

WAHB IBN MUNABBIH (d. 728). A devout Yemeni sage who introduced a large body of material into the commentary literature.

YĀQŪT (d. 1229). A historian of Hama in Syria.

ZAJJĀJ (d. 928). An early ḥadīth scholar with an interest in Qur'ānic commentary.

CHAPTER ONE

The Life of Mary 🌸

THE Qur'ān describes itself as a 'warner', a 'guide' and a "clarifier", not as a chronicle,[1] and for this reason we should not expect to find in it a detailed biography of any of the great historical and prophetic figures it mentions. Muslim scholars have characteristically analysed not the detailed facts of her life, but the 'meaning of Mary', as this indeed seems to be the focus of the texts given in the Qur'ān.

Nonetheless, there has been a great deal of interesting discussion within the vast body of classical Sunni texts surrounding Mary which has endeavoured both to clarify and to fill out further the picture supplied by the Qur'ān. In this realm of clarification and inclusion of missing data, one finds the scholars relying on a wide spectrum of sources, particularly from the traditions or ḥadīths of the Prophet Muḥammad (ﷺ) that are technically classified as 'sound' (ṣaḥīḥ), or 'good' (ḥasan), or those which are questionable, or which at times are apparently fictional stories. When the data are considered questionable from the perspective of Islam because they are based on the so-called Israelitic (Isrā'īlī) sources (Christian and Jewish sources), we find that the scholars at times accept them with reservations or reject them with reservations, basing their analysis on the following Qur'ānic passage and the commentary on it by the Prophet Muḥammad (ﷺ) found in the collection of ḥadīth known as the *Ṣaḥīḥ* of al-Bukhārī:

> We believe in God, and in that which was revealed unto us and that which was revealed unto Abraham and Ishmael and Isaac and Jacob and the Tribes, and that which Moses and Jesus received, and that which the Prophets received from their Lord. We make no distinction between any of them, and unto Him we have surrendered. (2:136)[2]

> It is narrated that Abū Hurayra said: 'The People of the Book [*Ahl al-Kitāb*][3] were reading the Torah in Hebrew and explaining it in Arabic to the Muslims, so the Messenger of God (ﷺ) said: "Neither believe the Ahl al-Kitāb nor believe them to be lying; say:" [and he recited Qur'ān 2:136].' (al-Bukhārī)[4]

As for the stories which may be classed simply as fictional, these are valuable not as sources of fact, but as further illustrations of the Marian idea in traditional Islam; in other words, they serve the same purpose as a novel or a poem which intensifies meaning and animates its heroes and heroines. Some of these tales will be analysed in this light in subsequent chapters. At present, however, our concern is to document traditional Sunni Islam's view of the events of Mary's life. The data has been sifted by traditional scholarly discussions about enigmatic or extra-Qur'ānic data—details about her background, her mother's vow, her birth and guardianship, the birth of Jesus (ﷺ), their flight from Herod, and finally her death and attainment of Paradise.

Her Parents: Ḥanna's Vow

> [Remember] when the wife of ʿImrān . . . (3:35)
> And Mary, the daughter of ʿImrān . . . (66:12)

The Qur'ān informs us that the father of Mary was named ʿImrān, and the classical Muslim scholars unanimously accept that she was from the line of the prophet David (ﷺ). Differences of opinion emerge, however, over the intervening genealogy, most probably due to a lack of familiarity with such foreign names and consequent error in recording them in the Arabic orthography. According to the Spanish exegete al-Qurṭubī, 'All of these differences are mentioned because the Prophets and Messengers are all descendants one of the other.'[5] The following genealogy (taking into account orthographic variations), which is attributed to Ibn Isḥāq or directly to the Prophet's (ﷺ) companion Ibn ʿAbbās, is the most generally accepted: Mary bint ʿImrān ibn Yāshim ibn Mīshā ibn Hazqiyā ibn Yāwish (ibn Īshā ibn Yahushāfat) ibn Sulaymān ibn Dāwūd (ﷺ).[6] Although the name of her mother is not supplied by the Qur'ān, it is universally accepted as Ḥanna bint Fāqūdh.[7]

Ibn Isḥāq[8] tells us that Ḥanna prayed to become pregnant with a male child, and then, when she became pregnant, she vowed that the child would be dedicated to the service of God at Bayt al-Maqdis (Jerusalem).[9]

> [Remember] when the wife of ʿImrān said: My Lord! I have vowed unto Thee that which is in my belly for Thy special service. Accept it from me. Lo! Thou, only Thou, art the Hearer, the Knower. (3:35)

Al-Ṭabarī adds that 'they claim' or 'in what they say', Ḥanna was past menopause and had no children; thus, when she became pregnant, she made the vow of consecration of the unborn babe.[10] Further background to Ḥanna's conception and consequent vow is found in the following account, included by several historians and commentators on the Qur'ān:

> It is related that Ḥanna was barren, and she was sitting in the shade of a tree when she saw a bird feeding its chicks, thus arousing in her the desire for a child, and she wished for him.[11]

Then, some say, she prayed: 'O Lord God, I make a vow that if Thou providest me with a child, I will grant him to the Temple [Bayt al-Maqdis]'. Others say that before making the vow, her husband ʿImrān asked her what she would do if it were a female child, and only then did she make the vow, although this is the less accepted view.[12] An additional event connected to the period of time during which Ḥanna was pregnant is the death of ʿImrān.[13] Although the death of Mary's father is not actually stated in the Qur'ān, it can be logically deduced from Zachariah's (ﷺ) assumption of Mary's guardianship, and thus generally accepted by traditional Sunni scholarship as fact.

The Birth of Mary and Her Guardianship

> And when she delivered, she said: My Lord! Lo! I am delivered of a female—And God knew best of what she delivered—The male is not as the female; and Lo! I have named her Mary and Lo! I crave Thy protection for her and her offspring from Satan the outcast. (Qur'ān, 3:36)
>
> And her Lord accepted her with full acceptance and vouchsafed to her a goodly growth; and made Zachariah her guardian. Whenever Zachariah went out to the sanctuary [*miḥrāb*] where she was he found her supplied with sustenance. He said: O Mary! Whence comes this to you? She said: It is from God. God provides sustenance to whom He pleases without measure. (Qur'ān, 3:37)
>
> This is part of the tidings of things unseen, which We reveal unto thee [Muḥammad]. Thou wast not with them when they cast lots with reeds [to know] which of them should be guardian of Mary, nor wast thou with them when they disputed [the point]. (Qur'ān, 3:44)

According to the classical exegetes it was customary at that time to consecrate boys to the Temple. They would stay at the Temple, worshipping there and serving it until puberty, at which time they could choose to continue their service or not. Thus Badawī, whose work relies on traditional Sunni scholarship, sees that Ḥanna, having given birth to a girl, views the statement in 3:36 as a request to God to excuse her from the vow she had made to consecrate her 'son' to the Temple.[14] Ḥanna, however, was bound to her vow even though the child was a girl. The following anecdote indicates the degree of solemnity of such a vow, in Islam:

> A man of the Sufi Way once told his mother: 'O Mother! Give me to God—that I may worship Him and learn the Knowledge'. She replied 'Yes'. So, he travelled until he began to rethink the matter; then he returned to her and knocked on her door. She said: 'Who is it?' 'It's your son, so-and-so', came the reply; but she said: 'We have left you to God, and we will not take you back.'[15]

The commentators record that even the name Mary, which Ḥanna gave to the child, is said to have had the meaning of '"The one who worships", in their language', which was Aramaic at that time,[16] a further indication of Ḥanna's dedication to her vow and of the nature of the future life of Mary.

Ḥanna, with the child wrapped in her shawl, set off for the Temple for two reasons: firstly, to carry out her vow to consecrate Mary to the Temple, and secondly, to find a suitable guardian for the child, whose father had died and who was a special case—a girl, the only female of the Israelites ever to have been so consecrated. It seems to be generally accepted by the classical Muslim scholars that Ḥanna did this shortly after Mary was born, although some commentators indicate that she was subsequently returned to Ḥanna or Zachariah's wife for the nursing period before actually beginning her devotions at the Temple.[17]

Ḥanna brought the baby to the 'scribe-rabbis'—called by some commentators 'the sons of Aaron'.[18] Going to their place of seclusion at Bayt al-Maqdis she announced, 'Yours she is, consecrated'. They then disputed over who would take responsibility for her as she was related to them and came from a family of worldly as well as religious leaders. Zachariah said: 'I have more right to her, as her aunt[19] is of my household.' At this point, the rabbis decided to cast lots for Mary's guardianship. According to ʿIkrīma, al-Suddī, Qatāda and al-Rabīʿ ibn Anas, this casting of lots took place at the River Jordan.[20] Some twenty-seven *aqlām*[21] were cast, and all of them sank (or drifted away with the current, in some versions), with the exception of that of Zachariah which rose to the surface of the water and was not carried away by the current, a clear sign from God that he was to be the guardian of this unique child. Thus God miraculously drew together Mary and Zachariah (ﷺ), the leader of the rabbis and a prophet in his own right, and in so doing, provided her with the best of spiritual guides.

Zachariah then constructed a sanctuary (*miḥrāb*)[22] for the small child, which could not be reached except by stairs, as Waḍḍāḥ al-Yaman said in verse:

> Lady of the *miḥrāb*; if I came to her
> I could not find her unless I climbed the stair.[23]

Zachariah alone entered Mary's *miḥrāb*, locking the door (or 'seven' doors, in most accounts) behind him when he departed. Whenever Zachariah, as Mary's guardian, came to provide her with food or drink, he was amazed to find that she had already been provided, not just with sustenance (*rizq*), but with the best of sustenance, including 'the fruit of winter in summer and the fruit of summer in winter'.[24] Zachariah, observing these miraculous provisions and being aware that the doors were always locked and that he had the only key, asked from whence came the food, and Mary, still speaking as a child, responded: 'It is from God . . . ' (Qur'ān, 3:37).[25] Related to this passage is an explicatory ḥadīth which is found in all the historians and Qur'ānic commentators:

> Sahl ibn Zanjala narrated on the authority of Jābir ibn ʿAbdullāh that the Messenger of God (ﷺ) went some days without eating anything until it became difficult, so he went to his wives' abodes, but he found nothing in the homes of any of them. So he went to Fāṭima and said: 'O my daughter, do you have anything to eat, as I am famished?' She said, 'No', pledging that she was speaking the truth. Then, after the Messenger of God (ﷺ) had left her house, a neighbour sent her two loaves of bread and a little meat, and she took them from her and put them in a bowl and covered it, saying: 'It is preferable to give it to the Messenger of God rather than to myself and my family'. And they were all in need of

food. She sent Ḥasan and Ḥusayn to their grandfather, who was the Messenger of God (ﷺ), and he returned to her, so she said: 'By you and my mother! O Messenger of God, God has given us something, and it came for you.' He said: 'Bring it to me.' And she brought it and lifted the cover of the bowl and found it full of bread and meat. And when she looked at him astonished, she knew that it was a blessing from God, the most High, and she gave thanks to Him. And the Prophet (ﷺ) said: 'It comes from God. Verily, God provides sustenance to whom He pleases without measure'; (3:37) and he said: 'Praise be to God Who has done for you something akin to what He did for the Lady [*sayyida*] of the Israelites'—that is to say, that God had provided her with the best of sustenance. She [Mary] was asked about it, and she said: 'It is from God. Verily He provides sustenance to whom He pleases without measure.' And the Prophet (ﷺ) sent for ʿAlī and he came to him, and the Messenger of God (ﷺ) and ʿAlī and Fāṭima and al-Ḥasan and al-Ḥusayn ate, and likewise all the wives of the Prophet (ﷺ), until they were sated, and there was still some remaining in the bowl. And Fāṭima said: 'I will give some to my neighbours'. Thus did God bestow many blessings and much good. The basis [of this feast] was two loaves of bread and a portion of meat, while the rest was a blessing from God, the most High. (Narrated by Abū Yaʿlā.)[26]

Upon seeing this recurring miracle, Zachariah was encouraged to pray to God that he and his barren wife in their old age[27] would likewise be blessed with a son, and the angel Gabriel informed him that he would be granted John (Yaḥyā) (3:38-40). Meanwhile, Mary continued her solitary worship in her *miḥrāb* until she reached the age of puberty.

The Birth of ʿĪsā ibn Maryam

[And remember] when the angels said: O Mary! Lo! God giveth thee glad tidings of a Word from Him, whose name

> is the Messiah Jesus the son of Mary, illustrious in the world and in the Hereafter, and one of those brought near [unto God]. (3:45)
>
> She said: My Lord! How can I have a child when no mortal hath touched me? He said: So [it shall be]. God createth what He will. If He decreeth a thing, He saith unto it only: Be! and it is. (3:47)

Mary attained puberty, and she began to stay with Zachariah's wife during the courses of her menstruation, and after completing the menstrual cycle and performing the *ghusl* (the major ritual ablution, which entails the washing of the whole body), she would return, ritually pure, to her *miḥrāb*.[28] Mary increased in worship until there was no person known at that time who approached her in the time of worshipping.[29] Being physically capable at this stage in her development, Mary began her service at the Temple. It is at this point that Joseph (Yūsuf) the Carpenter begins to appear in the accounts of her life. However since Joseph is never mentioned in the Qur'ān or ḥadīth material, the information supplied concerning him, and especially about his connection with Mary, is expressed with extreme caution. Such accounts are either concluded with a prudent '*wa'Llāhu a ʿlam*' ('and God knows best') or prefaced with the words 'it is said', or 'they say' (the identity of the source being left unspecified) or, at times, 'Christian sources say'. The following discussion can hence be no more than an attempt to clarify the elements which recur with the most frequency and appear to have been most widely acquiesced in by Islamic scholarship.

Joseph is said to have been Mary's cousin,[30] a carpenter who was also in service at the Temple. As a result, he became aware of Mary's devoutness and the palpable excellence of her worship. They both made use of a source of water in a grotto on the Mount of Olives (Jabal al-Zaytūn).[31] Then there is a solitary account found in Ibn Hishām's Sīra (biography of the Prophet), and attributed to Ibn Isḥāq. This account implies a second casting of lots:

> It was Jurayj the priest, a man of the Israelites, a carpenter, whose arrow separated out, who took responsibility for Mary. And it was Zachariah who had been her guardian before this time. The Israelites had suffered a terrible calamity, and Zachariah had grown too old to bear the responsibility of Mary; thus they cast lots for her, and Jurayj the priest won, and took the responsibility.[32]

The same account is found in Thaʿlabī's collection of prophetic biographies (*Qiṣaṣ*), still uniquely attributed to Ibn Isḥāq, except this time it is Joseph the Carpenter who casts lots and gains responsibility for the guardianship of Mary.[33] Due to the solitary attestation of this anecdote, the lack of reference to it in the Qur'ān and ḥadīth, and the confusion of identities in the two versions, it must be discarded as unreliable. In fact, in traditional Muslim sources Joseph's relationship with Mary is frequently not clarified, or he is mentioned as her companion and relation only, because there is no revealed basis for anything more specific, such as the statement that he was her fiancé and later became her husband, both of which are generally attributed to the Gospels, if mentioned at all.[34] Ibn al-Qayyim further claims that Mary and Joseph were from different tribes and thus could not have been married to each other as this was against Jewish law.[35]

> And make mention of Mary in the Scripture, when she withdrew from her people to a place looking East. (Qur'ān, 19:16)
>
> She placed a screen [to obscure herself] from them. Then We sent unto her Our Spirit and it assumed for her the likeness of a perfect man. (Qur'ān, 19:17)

The Virgin is thought to have been between ten and fifteen years of age, and to have had two menstrual periods at the time of the miraculous conception.[36] At this time she withdrew from her people to an eastern part of Jerusalem (probably just outside the Temple area): Ṭabarī records that the East is traditionally the most preferred place spiritually as it is the direction from which light emanates. Then, according to Mujāhid, al-Ḍaḥḥāk, Qatāda, Ibn Jarīr, Wahb ibn Munabbih and al-Suddī, *rūḥanā*, 'Our Spirit', namely the angel Gabriel (ﷺ) (Jibrīl) was sent to Mary by God.[37] The *qiṣaṣ* literature and some of the histories include a story elaborating on these events. It relates how Mary requests that Joseph accompany her to fetch water from the grotto; but as he does not need water, she ventures there alone, to find the angel Gabriel already present when she arrives; or, on one account, he appears after her arrival. This material does not appear in the major commentaries,[38] perhaps because it lacks a chain of authorities (*isnād*) and seems generally incongruous with the Qur'ānic account and with Mary's personality. In another version of this event, which Ṭabarī includes in both his Qur'ānic commentary (*Jāmiʿ*) and his *Annals (Tārīkh)*, the implication is that the incident described in the first part of 19:17 took place at a different time from the rest of this passage; in other words, Mary's screening of herself was not connected to the appearance of Gabriel:

> Suddī said, on the authority of Ibn ʿAbbās and Ibn Masʿūd and some of the other Companions, that the Prophet (ﷺ) said: 'Mary went out [to a place] to one side of the *miḥrāb* because of her menstrual period. And she set up a screen [to conceal herself from them], a screen of the walls [i.e. she screened herself behind the walls].'[39]

If this is true, it indicates that 19:16 and the two parts of 19:17 are disconnected in time, as she clearly did not have the experience of the miraculous conception during the monthly cycle. A more likely possibility, however, is that these two texts are indeed a description of connected events: when Mary withdrew and screened herself from public view, she was acting (consciously or intuitively, or from divine inspiration) in preparation for the coming of the angel, especially as it was accepted that she went to stay with the wife of Zachariah during the menstrual period and returned to the Temple only when ritually pure. The matter is still a point of some debate.

She said: Lo! I seek refuge in the Beneficent One from thee, if thou art God-fearing. (Qur'ān, 19:18)

He said: I am only a messenger of thy Lord, to bestow upon thee the gift of a holy son. (Qur'ān, 19:19)

She said: How can I have a son when no mortal hath touched me, neither have I been unchaste? (Qur'ān, 19:20)

He said: So [it shall be]. The Lord saith: It is easy for Me. And we shall make him a Sign for mankind and a Mercy from Us; and it is a thing ordained. (Qur'ān, 19:21)

So, she conceived him, and she withdrew with him to a far place. (Qur'ān, 19:22)

And she who was chaste: And We breathed into her [something] of Our Spirit and made her and her son a token for [all] peoples. (Qur'ān, 21:91)

And Mary the daughter of 'Imrān, whose womb was chaste: And We breathed therein something of Our Spirit . . . (Qur'ān, 66:12)

When Mary had withdrawn to 'the Eastern part' of Jerusalem, the angel Gabriel appeared in the form of 'a perfect man' in order not to shock her with his true angelic form, so that she would be able to accept what he was about to tell her.[40] Nevertheless, Mary the Pure was frightened and prayed to her Lord for protection from this seeming mortal, who was an apparent stranger. Gabriel then explained who he was and the nature of his mission from God. Upon hearing this news, Mary surrendered immediately to the will of her Lord, and Gabriel breathed 'of the Spirit of God'[41] into the pit (of the sleeve) of her garment, and at God's command: '*kun fa yakūn*' ('Be! And it is'), she conceived.[42]

Two dialogues which are said to have occurred just after the conception are recorded in almost all traditional accounts of the Virgin's life. One is an exchange between Mary and the wife of Zachariah, and the other is a conversation which takes place between Mary and Joseph. Their respective reactions to the awareness of the pregnancy of Mary present striking contrasts. On one hand, the first account, which is a follow-up to the account cited earlier in which Mary screens herself during menstruation, states that after conception, the following took place:

> Suddī narrates that Mary's sister, who was wife to Zachariah, came to her one night in order to visit her, and when she opened the door to enter, she said: 'I sense that I am with child'. Zachariah's wife replied: 'I find what is in my belly prostrating to what is in your belly'.[43]

Thus, Zachariah's wife implicitly accepts Mary's miraculous conception without questioning her, which is not excessively surprising, as her own conception of the prophet John or Yaḥyā (عليه السلام) when she was an old, barren woman past the age of childbearing had been miraculous too. Joseph, on the other hand, in spite of his awareness of Mary's immaculate character, had to be convinced because he, unlike ʿAshyāʾ (Elizabeth), had no previous experience of miracles:

> According to Wahb ibn Munabbih, there was with Mary in the mosque a good man of her family, called Joseph the Carpenter who like her was a servant at the Temple. This man, when he beheld her heavy belly and her greatness, found it to be a strange matter; then he considered his knowledge of her piety, her righteousness, purity, respectability, her religiosity and her worship, and, having considered deeply, reached the conclusion that this was a matter that he himself was unable to fathom. So he determined to speak to her about it, and he said: 'O Mary, I desire to ask you about a matter.' She said: 'What is it?' He said: 'Has there ever been a tree without a seed? And has there ever been a plant without a seed? And has there ever been a child without a father?' She said: 'Yes'—and she understood to what thing he was alluding. 'As to your question about the tree and the plant, well, in the first instance, God created the tree and the plant without seeds. And as to your question of whether there has ever been a child without a father, well, God, the Most High,

> created Adam without either father or mother.' Thus Joseph believed her, and found no blame in her condition.[44]

But not everyone was convinced, and some began to make suspicious accusations about the cause of her condition, so Mary, the Faithful, withdrew to a place far away from them.

> Then, the pangs of childbirth drove her unto the trunk of the palm tree. She said: Oh, would that I had died before this and had become a thing forgotten and out of sight.
>
> Then [one] cried unto her from below her, saying: Grieve not! Thy Lord hath placed a rivulet beneath thee.
>
> And shake the trunk of the palm tree toward thee, thou wilt cause ripe dates to fall upon thee.
>
> So eat and drink and be consoled [lit.: 'cool thine eye']. And if thou meetest any mortal, say: Lo! I have vowed a fast unto the Beneficent, and may not speak this day to any mortal. (19:23-26)

There is no clear statement amongst the traditional Sunni scholars about the length of time which separated the miraculous conception from the birth of Jesus, although the general trend of opinion seems to support the twofold assessment of Ibn ʿAbbās. Firstly, Ibn ʿAbbās, contends that 'the matter is only that she was pregnant and delivered,' meaning that what is important is the miraculous nature of the event; and secondly that the whole process probably took about an 'hour' or a 'while' (*sāʿa*), because the events are mentioned consecutively in the Qur'ān. The compiler of Prophetic biographies al-Najjār adds that as the whole of the pregnancy was a miracle, there is no reason why the length of time should not also be a miracle.[45] In addition, some sources record the possibility that the pregnancy lasted one hour, the labour one hour and the delivery a further hour, this view being attributed to the second-century commentator Muqātil. There also exist other conjectures to the effect that it ranged between six and eight months.[46]

The labour pains drove Mary to a palm tree somewhere in the vicinity of Jerusalem, where she gave birth to Jesus.[47] Some of the scholars say that his birth took place in Nazareth (al-Nāṣira). The historians Ibn Saʿd, Yāqūt and Ibn ʿAsākir state that the Messiah was born in the vicinity of Nazareth, which is why his companions are called Nazarenes, and Jesus himself has been called a Nazarene, whence the word *Naṣārā*, the correct Arabic term for Christians.[48] Yāqūt adds that the people of Jerusalem reject this, claiming that the Messiah was born in Bethlehem (Bayt Laḥm) of which fact they have manifest proof, and that his mother carried him from Bethlehem to Nazareth.[49] Those scholars who accept this location quote Wahb ibn Munabbih as stating that the labour pains and the childbirth occurred 'between six and eight miles' from Jerusalem in a village called Bayt Laḥm (Bethlehem).[50] The Egyptian polymath al-Suyūṭī informs us that the Prophet's Companion ʿAbdullāh ibn ʿAmr ibn al-ʿĀṣ used to send lamp oil to Bethlehem where Jesus was born,[51] and both Suyūṭī and the Qur'ānic commentator Ibn Kathīr cite an authenticated ḥadīth from the collection of al-Nasā'ī in which during the Night Journey and Ascension *(al-Isrā' wa'l-Miʿrāj)*,[52] Gabriel instructs the Prophet Muḥammed (ﷺ) to pray in various places and asks him if he knows where he has prayed. One of the places is 'Bethlehem, the place where ʿĪsā was born'.[53]

Suffering from false accusations, Mary cried out to her Lord, and as a mercy to her, a voice cried out to her 'from below' indicating the miraculous appearance of food and drink and commanding the Virgin to fast. Many of the scholars, including Ṭabarī, are of the opinion that the voice from below was that of the Archangel, and that Jesus did not speak until Mary brought him to her people.[54] The miraculous nature of the event is further confirmed by the fact that palm trees of the type beneath which she sat do not bear fruit; furthermore it was winter, when even fruit-bearing trees are dormant.[55]

The subsequent reference to Mary fasting from food and speech[56] is said to denote a contemporary custom. Qurṭubī quotes the following ḥadīth to show that this was Israelite custom even at the time of the Prophet Muḥammed (ﷺ). This ḥadīth, together with two others, indicates that although fasting from food and speech had been customary, it was rejected by the Prophet (ﷺ) for his *umma* (the community of Islam); however, abstinence from undesirable speech while fasting remains essential for a sincere Muslim:

> Ibn ᶜAbbās narrated: While the prophet (ﷺ) was delivering a sermon, he saw a man standing, so he asked about that man. They said: 'It is Abū Isrā'īl who has vowed that he will stand and never sit down, and never be in the shade nor speak to anyone while he is fasting.' The Prophet (ﷺ) said: 'Order him to speak,and let him come in the shade, and let him sit down, and let him complete his fast.' (Narrated by Bukhārī)[57]

> The Prophet (ﷺ) said: 'If one of you is fasting; then he must not behave obscenely or ignorantly. Thus, if he is ordered to slay or to curse someone, then let him say: I am fasting.' (Narrated by Bukhārī and Muslim)[58]

> Abū Hurayra narrated that the Messenger of God (ﷺ) said: 'He who does not give up false speech and the telling of lies, then God has no need for him to give up his food and his drink.' (Bukhārī)[59]

According to the *qiṣaṣ* literature, a parallel event to this miraculous pregnancy of Mary (ﷺ) and the subsequent birth of Jesus (ﷺ) was the death of Zachariah (ﷺ). Thaᶜlabī mentions two accounts of this event, one of which is attributed to Kaᶜb al-Aḥbār, in which the cause of Zachariah's distraught condition and flight from his people is identified with the death of his son John (the prophet Yaḥyā ﷺ). This should probably be dismissed, since the previous discussion about the birth of John indicated that he would have been an infant at this time, or a child of three years, or, at most, could not have more than fifteen years old. As the Qur'ān clearly indicates that Zachariah was encouraged to pray for a son as a result of seeing the miraculous sustenance that God provided for Mary, who is thought to have been between ten and fifteen years old at the time of conception, that would eliminate the possibility that

John would have been established as a prophet at this time and as a helper to Jesus, also an infant, or not yet born, and hence he could not have met his death at this time and thereby been the cause of Zachariah's distraction.

The second account mentioned by Thaʿlabī and others contains some more plausible elements. In this account, Zachariah fled from his people because he was falsely accused of adultery as he had been the sole person to enter Mary's *miḥrāb*. 'It is said that the reason for Zachariah's murder was that the devil[60] attended the meeting of the Israelite elders and accused Zachariah of Mary's pregnancy, as he was the only one to have entered the *miḥrāb*.'[61]

The Qur'ānic account continues:

> Then she brought him to her own folk, carrying him. They said: O Mary! Thou hast come with an amazing thing.
>
> O sister of Hārūn (Aaron)! Thy father was not a wicked man nor was thy mother a harlot. (19:27–28)

Returning to the events directly associated with the birth of Jesus, after giving birth, Mary walked, carrying the infant back to her people. Upon seeing her with this child, and having no knowledge of her having married anyone, they slandered her using the epithet: '*yā ukhta Hārūn*' ('O sister of Aaron').[62]

In an effort to make sure that the ignorant amongst the believers do not make the error of assuming that Mary was the actual sister of Aaron (عليه السلام), the Qur'ānic commentators first stress the huge time span between the eras in which the two lived. Then they suggest possible interpretations, with al-Suddī proposing, for example, that Mary actually had a brother on her father's side. But, although without any factual data any interpretation is possible, and since it was Mary's mother Ḥanna who desperately prayed for the child rather than her father ʿImrān, a second explanation seems much more likely. It is said that the meaning of the verse is: 'O you who are similar to Aaron in your pious worship of God', and thus the statement becomes a reprimand to her for having borne the child without being married, a shocking sin given her position at the Temple and the known righteousness of her immediate family and her ancestors.[63] The commentators strengthen their case with the inclusion of a ḥadīth in which the Prophet (ﷺ) himself clarifies the meaning:

> Al-Mughīra ibn Shuʿba said: 'When I arrived at Najrān,[64] they [the Christians] questioned me, saying: "You (Muslims) recite: 'O sister of Aaron' and Moses was before Jesus by such-and-such a period;" so when I approached the Messenger of God (ﷺ), I asked him about that, and he said that they used to call themselves after the Prophets and righteous people that preceded them.' (Narrated by Muslim)[65]
>
> Then she pointed to him. They said: How can we talk to one who is in a cradle, a young boy? (Qur'ān, 19:29)
>
> He spoke: Lo! I am the slave of God. He hath given me the scripture and hath appointed me a Prophet. (19:30)
>
> And hath made me blessed wheresoever I may be, and hath enjoined upon me prayer and almsgiving so long as I remain alive. (19:31)
>
> And [hath made me] kindly dutiful to my mother, and hath not made me arrogant or troublesome. (19:32)

To return for a moment to the period immediately preceding the birth of Jesus, it should be noted that the Central Asian exegete al-Zamakhsharī includes a report stating that Joseph the Carpenter took Mary and her child to a cave, where they stayed for forty days until the afterbirth period was complete. Then she brought the child to her people.[66] The modern writer ʿAbd al-Salām Badawī rejects this claim based on a literal understanding of Mary's purity which would rule out the possibility of her bleeding after birth.[67] The Qur'ān itself, however, suggests a further possible reason for rejecting the supposition that Mary stayed in the cave for forty days. If we consider the text at 19:26 in which Mary, the Obedient, was ordered to vow a fast from food and speech for a day, and 19:29 in which, when she brought the babe to her people and they made their accusations, she did not speak but pointed to him instead, the indication appears to be that the vow and the pointing occurred on the same day.

Next, God miraculously allows the new-born infant to speak, thereby redeeming his mother by exposing the baby's relationship to God as His slave and Prophet. For those who believed, Jesus's speaking in the cradle clarified what had seemed inexplicable to some and despicable to others—but not all did so.

The Flight from Herod

Thaʿlabī's account affirms that 'Jesus was born forty-two years from the time of King Augustus and fifty-one years had passed since the time of al-Ashkanbīn,'[68] and at that time, Julius Caesar, the king of Rome, was in power, and Herod was king of the Jews.[69] When Herod heard about the Messiah, he was determined to kill him, but, according to Ṭabarī, God commanded the angel to tell Joseph the Carpenter, who was with Mary in the Temple, of Herod's intentions, and commanded Joseph to flee with the child and his mother.[70]

> And We made the son of Mary and his mother a sign. And We gave them both refuge on a height, a place of rest and water-springs. (Qur'ān, 23:50)

The scholars preface their commentary on this text by addressing two basic issues. The first questions the exact meaning of the phrase: *rabwatin dhāt qarārin wa maʿīn,* while the second considers its location. There is a consensus of opinion that the phrase means 'a high place on level ground, which is a good place due to its fertility and the availability of visible, flowing water', that is, water on the surface, not underground. However no agreement exists concerning the location of this *rabwa*. The scholars include a discussion of various possibilities, but without expressing a preference. It is hence possible that Mary and Jesus fled with Joseph from Bethlehem to another location in Palestine (near either Jerusalem or Ramla), or they fled to Damascus, or to Egypt.[71]

The suggestion that the location was near Jerusalem, and that it was the same place in which Mary had suffered the pains of childbirth, is based on an analysis which interprets the Qur'ān by using other Qur'ānic passages. On the other hand, the suggestion that it was Ramla is based on the ḥadīth (narrated by Abū Ḥātim on the authority of Murra al-Bahdhī), in which the Messenger of God (ﷺ) said to a man: 'Indeed, you will die in the *rabwa*'—and this man died at Ramla. Ibn Kathīr technically classes this ḥadīth as *gharīb* ('strange'), and Ṭabarī adds that Ramla does not have the basic characteristics described in 23:50.[72]

Ibn Kathīr's discussion about the possibility of Damascus being the site of the *rabwa* reads as follows:

> Ibn Abī Ḥātim narrated on the authority of Isrā'īl, on the authority of Mamāk, on the authority of ʿIkrīma, on the authority of Ibn ʿAbbās, that [the location described in] *dhāt qarārin wa maʿīn* is the river of Damascus and its surroundings. And Layth ibn Abī Sulaym said on the authority of Mujāhid that this verse refers to the time when Jesus son of Mary and his mother were given refuge in the Ghūṭa [a fertile area on the south side of Damascus] and its surroundings.[73]

Suyūṭī reproduces a ḥadīth narrated by al-Ḥasan ibn Shajjāʿ ar-Rabīʿ on the authority of ʿAlī ibn Abī Ṭālib about a man who questions the Prophet about Mount Qāsiyūn (outside Damascus). The Prophet says: 'And on it [Mount Qāsiyūn], Jesus son of Mary and his mother were given refuge.' Suyūṭī adds that:

> Whoever goes there must not shorten his prayer and his *duʿā'* [supererogatory prayers] because it is the place where prayers are answered, and whoever wishes to visit [the site of] *rabwatin dhāt qarārin wa maʿīn*, let him go to the highest peak between the two rivers, and climb up to the cave upon Mount Qāsiyūn, and pray there, as it is the house of Jesus and his mother when they took refuge from the Jews.[74]

Yāqūt gives a description of the greater area, the Ghūṭa:

> The area which includes Damascus, eighteen miles around Damascus, with high mountains on all sides, and in the northern part of it. Its mountains are very high, and the area

contains various rivers, thus producing forests and vegetation—it is one of the most beautiful places for scenery.[75]

The third possibility is that Mary, Jesus and Joseph fled from Herod to Egypt, and this version rests primarily upon Christian traditions. The Egyptian historian al-Maqrīzī refers to *Kitāb as-Sankasār* for much of his information about the details of the itinerary and the events.[76] Badawī relies on the material found in al-Maqrīzī's text and on a map which he says he found in the Church of the Two Saints Abākir and Yūḥannā in old Cairo and which outlines their route.[77] According to Maqrīzī's source, they first stopped in the city of Busṭa; then on to Qus (Qūsiya); then westward to Mir (Dayr al-Muḥriq). At this point Joseph has a dream in which a voice tells him that since Herod has died he must return with Mary and Jesus to al-Quds (Jerusalem). They stop at Qaṣr ash-Shamʿ and stay in a cave which subsequently became known as the Church of Busraja; then on to ʿAyn Shams in present-day Cairo. At ʿAyn Shams while Mary was washing the clothing of Jesus, she wrung the water out, and from the drops that fell on the ground, a balm (*balsan/balsam*) tree grew,[78] which is there today, and whose oil is still used by monks and others. Maqrīzī adds that the Copts all agree that the holy family also stopped at Bahnasā on their way back to al-Quds.[79] The modern writer Badawī first mentions the same places as al-Maqrīzī, and then goes on to discuss the map. He traces the route from al-ʿArīsh to Qūsiya, the site of Dayr al-Muḥriq. He avers that they left al-ʿArīsh on an unusual route to Farama; then to Tall Basṭa; then to Bilbays (near modern Zāgazīg); then to Samannūd; then west to al-Maḥalla al-Kubrā; then north to a resting place in Kafr ash-Shaykh; then westward to the eastern part of Wādī Natrūn; then south to ʿAyn Shams, the site of the miraculous balm tree. The actual map Badawī cites is found in the new edition of *The Holy Family in Egypt* by Otto Meinardus.[80]

Thaʿlabī adds, on the authority of Wahb ibn Munabbih, that

when Jesus was twelve years old, God the Most High revealed to Mary that Herod had died and ordered her to return with her cousin Joseph the Carpenter, to al-Shām,[81] which they did, and they settled in Nazareth.[82]

The Death of Mary (🌸)

And their statement that 'we killed the Messiah, Jesus son of Mary, God's Messenger'—while they killed him not nor crucified him, but so it was made to appear to them; and lo! those who disagree concerning it are in doubt thereof; they have no knowledge thereof save pursuit of conjecture; they killed him not for certain. (Qur'ān, 4:157)

But God raised him up unto Himself; God is ever Mighty, Wise. (Qur'ān, 4:158)

Little is known about the life of Mary after the return to Palestine. Ṭabarī, attributing his information to Christian sources, records that Mary lived for six years after Jesus was raised up, and that she was fifty and some years when she died. Badawī simply says that Mary lived on, worshipping God, after Jesus was taken up to the heavens.[83] However, Mary is included in some of the stories surrounding the events of the ascension of Jesus which are found in the *qiṣaṣ* and also in some of the histories.

The account which the historian Ibn al-Athīr includes in his *Tārīkh* is characteristic. It begins with the Qur'ānic statement, and then elaborates the missing details:

God sent angels who intervened and replaced Jesus with another man who looked like him on the cross. And God raised up the Messiah, after he had caused him to lose consciousness for three hours (and it is also said, for seven hours); then He revived him and raised him up. Then God said: Go down to Mary, as there is no-one who cries the tears she cries for you and no-one who suffers as does she. So he came down to her after seven days, and the mountain blazed with fire when light fell upon it, and she was at the cross crying, and with her was a woman who had been freed of possession by *jinns* [madness]. And he asked: What

> is the matter with you two? They said: [Is it] you? He said: God raised me up to Him and nothing but good has befallen me, and this matter was only something 'which was made to appear so to them. Then he ordered her to gather the Apostles, and he sent them as messengers for God around the land and ordered them to spread what God had commanded him with; then God raised him up to Him and covered him with light and prohibited him from the taste of food and drink, and he flew with the angels. Thus, he is with them; thus he became a being, angelic, heavenly, earthly.[84]

Thaʿlabī's account, which is attributed to Wahb ibn Munabbih, portrays Jesus before being raised up ordering two of the Apostles, Simon Peter[85] and John, to assume responsibility for his mother and not to part from her. She voyages with a group of the Apostles to a place somewhere in the Roman Empire, where Simon Peter and Andrew are killed and burned upside down, but Mary and John flee. However they are pursued, so the earth opens up for them, and they disappear. Mārūt,[86] the king of the Roman Empire, digs but cannot find their bodies. Thus realising the miraculous nature of the event, the king surrenders to the true religion of God.[87] Ibn al-Athīr includes a story in which the Apostles go to Herod, the king of the Roman Empire, who finally converts. In this narrative, however, there is no mention of Mary accompanying the Apostles, or of her being under the responsibility of John, or of her miraculous death.[88] Ibn Isḥāq mentions that according to Christian sources, the apostle John travelled to Ephesus after Jesus was raised up.[89] These stories may originate from the *Gospel of Nicodemus: Acts of Pilate* in which it is said that Pontius Pilate, the Roman procurator of Judaea, a ruthless governor, became a Christian. The *Gospel of Nicodemus* (300–500) was influential in the Middle Ages, and along with other Gospels was probably translated into Arabic and Syriac.[90] From the perspective of traditional Sunni Islam, of course, none of these accounts could be considered reliable sources for factual information about the death of Mary.

We turn now to the burial place of Mary. Suyūṭī repeatedly states that she lies in the well-known church, the Jasmāniyya (of Gethsemane),[91] which is located in the eastern district of Jerusalem near the foot of the Mount of Olives (Jabal al-Zaytūn). He does not, however, give any basis for his assumption. Ibn ʿAsākir places her grave in Damascus. He says: 'Whoever wants to see the grave of Maryam bint ʿImrān and the Apostles, them let them go to the cemetery of al-Farādīs (al-Daḥdāḥ), and this is the cemetery of Damascus'.[92]

Finally, as to the afterlife of Mary, it is the universal verdict of Islam that it is in Paradise. The classical ḥadīth commentary discussed in chapter four below reveals a strong preference for the belief that she is promised the highest status of all the ladies there. The following ḥadīth which al-Qurṭubī said had been passed down to him, emphasises this great importance of Mary in Islam:

> The Prophet said: 'If I were to swear, I would swear an oath that no-one shall enter Paradise before the early members of my *umma* (the community of all Muslims) except a few [*biḍʿat ʿashar*; i.e., from eleven to nineteen people], among whom are Abraham and Ishmael and Isaac and Jacob and *al-asbāṭ* (the Tribes' Founders), and Moses and Jesus, and Mary, the daughter of ʿImrān.'[93]

The following poem concludes this chapter on the life of Mary, summarising the main points and serving as a prelude to the discussions of her role as a mother, as the symbol of submission, as the Pure, the Best of Women, and the *ṣiddīqa* (the woman of true righteousness):[94]

Umayya[95] mentioned this account in his poetry:

And in your *dīn*,[96] God, *Subḥanallāh*,[97] the Lord of Mary,
made Mary and the slave,
Jesus son of Mary, a Sign, Clear Proof.
Mary, who turned in penitence to her Lord,
lived thereupon in chastity,
and He exalted her above the carping crowd.

She had no wish nor even thought of marriage,
nor passion nor even innocent company
with men.
So Mary lived, apart from any guardian kin,
dwelling alone for her Lord
at the land's edge of desolation,
Her presence veiled from the traveller by night and even so
by day.

A messenger from beyond this world and appetites, came down
while all else slept:
'Be not distressed, nor deny an angel from the Lord of ʿĀd[98] and
Jurhum.[99]
Heed and receive what you are asked to accept, for I am a
messenger from the Most Merciful, come with a son.'
Said Mary: 'How is this to be?
I am neither with child, nor wayward
nor a whore.
I give myself to the Most Merciful; if you be His messenger,
then sit or go.'
So he praised God and dazzled her, and breathing deep his breath,
deep to her cloak's pit.
By him she became with child; a matchless act!

And the Most Merciful never, never forsakes—
For when the babe was nigh, when Mary was to deliver,
God protected them
when those around her said:
'You have brought us a shocking thing.'
Thus it was in time that Jesus be protected and justified.
Mary had perception from her Lord and then, Mercy, by virtue
of the words of a prophet:
'I am a Sign from God, and He gave me Knowledge
and God is the Best of Teachers.
And I was sent [as a messenger] to mislead not,
nor trouble-make, nor was I sent through indecency:
nor was I sent through sin.'[100]

CHAPTER TWO

The Mother

Although exact details of Mary's daily life with her son Jesus (عليه السلام) are almost nonexistent in the Muslim sources, the nature of their relationship is indicated in the following ways. First of all, Jesus himself makes a declaration about his own life-long destiny and commitment to fulfil a duty of kindness and obedience to his mother, besides his obligation of responsibility for her well-being:

> And [hath made me] dutiful, kind to my mother and not arrogant or troublesome. (19:32)

Secondly, there is the implication of Mary's devotion to her son and his mission in her willingness to face her people with her child in spite of their aspersions on her character:

> And because of their disbelief and of their speaking against Mary grave, false accusations. (4:156)
>
> Then she brought him to her own folk, carrying him. They said: O Mary! Thou hast come with an amazing thing. (19:27)
>
> O sister of Aaron! Thy father was not a wicked man nor was thy mother a harlot. (19:28)[101]

In the period of exile from her homeland, the image of Mary portrayed by the Muslim classical historians is one of total acceptance of her role as a mother. There is no mention of Mary lamenting her circumstances, even though such behaviour might be normal for an adolescent of her age, shunned by her own people and in an alien environment. On the contrary, she is presented as a dutiful mother who cares for her child in infancy and encourages him to face life with a steadfastness of faith as he grows up.[102] Finally, and most significantly, the Qur'ān states that God made Mary and Jesus, 'a sign for [all] peoples'. (21:91)[103] Hence, the two, mother and child, are bound together as one in their representation of the best of human virtues, among which is the reciprocation of concern and affection which God has decreed between parent and child:

> Your parents and your children: Ye know not which of them is nearer unto you in usefulness. (4:11)

Underpinning the great symbolic image of Mary the mother is the Islamic view of the duties and rewards which determine the relationship between parents and children in general, and mothers in particular.[104] The Qur'ān famously charges the Muslim with kindness and gratitude to parents:

> Worship none save God only—and be good to parents. (2:83)

> Give thanks unto Me and unto thy parents. (31:14)

> And show kindness unto parents, and unto kinsfolk and orphans, and the needy. (4:36)

In their discussions of these and similar passages in the Qur'ān, the traditional scholars indicate that verses 2:83 and 31:14 stress the importance of duty to parents because of the texts' syntactic linkage of the injunction to worship God with that of being kind to parents.[105] In addition to financial considerations, the commentators indicate that the practical implications of 'kindness' (*iḥsān*) to parents include polite speech, obedience, mercy, tenderness, loving compassion, and praying on their behalf, as well as befriending their loved ones and other similar virtues.[106]

The ḥadīths further specify that the responsibility to, and the concern for, the mother take precedence over that of other members of the family:

> Abū Hurayra narrated: A man came to the Messenger of God (ﷺ) and said: 'O Messenger of God! Who is more entitled to be treated with the best of companionship by me?' The Prophet (ﷺ) said: 'Your mother.' The man said: 'Then who?' The Prophet (ﷺ) said: 'Your mother.' The man further said: 'Then who?' The Prophet (ﷺ) said: 'Your mother.' The man said again: 'Then who?' The Prophet (ﷺ) said: 'Then, your father.' (Narrated by al-Bukhārī and Muslim)[107]

As a result of the wide acceptance of this ḥadīth and the fact that the Prophet (ﷺ) stated 'Your mother' three times, Ibn Ḥajar ends his commentary on this Prophetic report with the Sufi author al-Muḥāsibī's statement that there is general consensus (*ijmāʿ*) amongst traditional Sunni Muslim scholars that the mother takes preference over the father in terms of the child's obligation to show concern and respect to his parents.[108] The following three ḥadīths relate the importance of the mother in Islam to the vital duties of liberative war (*jihād*)[109] and filial piety:

> Ibn Abī Awfā narrated that the Messenger of God (ﷺ) said: 'Know that Paradise is under the shade of the sword.' (al-Bukhārī; Aḥmad ibn Ḥanbal; Muslim; al-Tirmidhī)[110]

> ʿAbdullāh ibn ʿAmr [ibn al-ʿĀṣ] said: A man once came to the Prophet (ﷺ) asking his permission to go on *jihād*, and he asked, 'Are your parents alive?' The man said: 'Yes'. He (ﷺ) then said: 'Then [struggling] in their service is your *jihād*.' (Muslim; al-Bukhārī; al-Nasā'ī; Abū Dāwūd; al-Tirmidhī)[111]

Shawkānī states that since this ḥadīth and other versions of it indicate that *jihād* (in the sense of the just war) is not a universal individual duty (*farḍ ʿayn*)[112] as it depends on parental consent; hence filial piety is a superior virtue. This would imply that at times when conscription is not required by the caliph or when the parent is dependent on the child, the Muslim thereby substitutes the *jihād* of the *nafs*[113] for the *jihād* against the *kuffār* by his struggle to please his parents. Shawkānī further defines the phrase *fa-jāhid* as meaning: 'what is a duty for others [i.e. *jihād* against the military enemy] should be replaced, in this case, by one's duty to parents'.[114]

> Muʿāwiya ibn Jāhima narrated that [his son] Jāhima went to the Prophet (ﷺ) and said: 'O Messenger of God, I want to fight, and I have come to ask your advice'. He (ﷺ) said: 'Do you have a mother?' and he replied that he did. 'Then, stay with her,' the Prophet told him, 'because Paradise is under her foot.' (al-Nasā'ī; Ibn Māja; al-Ḥākim and al-Ṭabarānī)[115]

These three ḥadīths hence demonstrate that the Muslim's fulfilment of the obligation to fight the outward *jihād* of warfare against oppression, and the obligation to the inward struggle to serve his parents' needs and wishes, are both doors to Paradise. But the ḥadīths clarify that duty to parents, especially to the mother, is of primary importance.

The basis for the special status of the Muslim mother is expressed in the following verse:

> And we have enjoined on human beings kindness toward parents. His mother beareth him with hardship, and bringeth him forth with hardship, and the bearing and the weaning of him is thirty months, until, when he attaineth full strength and reacheth forty years, he saith: My Lord: Arouse me that I may give thanks for the favour wherewith Thou hast favoured me and my parents, and that I may do right acceptable unto Thee. And be gracious unto me in the matter of my offspring. (46:15)

In addition, a Muslim woman's joyful compliance with her motherly duties affords her immense opportunities for spiritual reward, as the following ḥadīth illustrates:

> Anas narrated that Sallāma, the nurse of the Prophet's son Ibrāhīm, said to the Prophet (ﷺ): 'O Messenger of God,

you have brought tidings of all the good things to men, but not to women'. He said: 'Did your women friends put you up to asking me this question?' 'Yes, they did,' she replied, and he said: 'Does it not please any one of you that if she is pregnant by her husband and he is satisfied with that, she receives the reward of one who fasts and prays for the sake of God? And when the labour pains come no-one in the heavens or the earth knows what is concealed in her womb to delight her? And when she delivers, not a mouthful of milk flows from her and not a suck does she give, but that she receives, for every mouthful and every suck, the reward of one good deed. And if she is kept awake by her child at night, she receives the reward of one who frees seventy slaves for the sake of God.' (al-Ṭabarānī)[116]

Two additional ḥadīths specify the recompense for fasting for a day for the sake of God and freeing only one slave, thus emphasizing the great blessedness of the woman's fulfilment of the normal routine of maternal duties:

> Abū Saʿīd al-Khudrī said: 'I heard the Prophet (ﷺ) say: "Whoever fasts for one day for the sake of God, God will keep his face away from the Fire for seventy days".' (al-Bukhārī)[117]
>
> Abū Hurayra narrated: 'The Prophet (ﷺ) said: "Whoever liberates a Muslim slave, God will save for every limb [of the slave] one of his own limbs from Hellfire".' Saʿīd ibn Marjāna said: 'I told this to ʿAlī ibn al-Ḥusayn, who had intended to sell a slave of his, for whom ʿAbdullāh ibn Jaʿfar had offered ʿAlī ten thousand dirhams (or one thousand dinars), and he freed the slave.' (al-Bukhārī)[118]

The implication of these three ḥadīths is that by virtue of having borne the pain of childbirth and of having given herself to her child in its early years, the mother in traditional Islam is due the worldly reward of good treatment and respect of the highest order, as well as spiritual blessings that are much greater than those for one day's sincere fasting or for freeing one slave, acts which are themselves forms of protection from the Fire. This is not to say that every conscientious Muslim mother is automatically guaranteed Paradise, but rather that she greatly improves her chances by being so. The ultimate reward, according to Islamic doctrine, depends on a cumulative outweighing of bad deeds by good ones, along with doctrinal factors, such as faith in the Oneness of God and acceptance of His Prophets; and above all, it depends on God's mercy. The following texts are Qur'ānic passages which speak about the balancing of deeds on the Day of Judgement:

> And anyone who does an atom's weight of good shall see it then. And anyone who does an atom's weight of evil shall see it then. (99:7–8)

> Then, as for the one whose balance [of good deeds] is heavy; he will live a contented life [in Paradise]. But as for the one whose balance [of good deeds] is light, his destination shall be a chasm. And what will explain to thee what that is? [It is] a raging Fire. (101:6–11)

Other proof-texts speak of the divine mercy as the ultimate determining factor:

> And to God belongeth all that is in the heavens and in the earth. He forgiveth whom He will, and punisheth whom He will. And God is Oft-Forgiving, Most Merciful. (3:129)

Consequently, the Muslim tries to increase his good deeds and hence his prospects of salvation. One of the ways in which the Muslim mother attempts to do this is via the fulfilment of her responsibilities to her children throughout her lifetime. The Prophet (ﷺ) indicates the spiritual blessings for this endeavour in the following ḥadīth:

> ʿĀ'isha, the wife of the Prophet (ﷺ), once related: 'A lady accompanied by her two daughters came to me asking for alms, but she did not find anything with me except one date, which I gave to her, and she divided it between the two daughters and got up and went away. The Prophet (ﷺ) came in and I told him what had taken place. He said:

> "Whoever is in charge of daughters and treats them generously, then, they will act as a shield for him from the fire".' (al-Bukhārī; Muslim and al-Tirmidhī)[119]

Despite the fact that Islam extols the role of motherhood in general, and specifically designates Mary as 'a sign to all peoples,' and hence a key symbol of female virtue, our sources offer hardly any discussion about her maternal role as such. Three possible explanations for this seeming lack of emphasis might be suggested.

The first lies in the basic importance to Islam of focussing on the child-parent aspect of the relationship, because clarification of the status of Jesus is pivotal to Islamic doctrine. Thus, Jesus is referred to as the 'son of Mary' because he has no father.[120] The Qur'ān stresses this relationship in the Chapter of Mary verse 32, where Jesus speaks in the cradle and defines his projected relationship with his mother. Ibn Kathīr sees this passage as a comparison between man's obedience to Allah and his respect for his parents in general, and more specifically as an indication of Mary's total rights over her son, as he has no other parent.[121] An account attributed to Wahb ibn Munabbih which relates an event said to have taken place in Egypt when Jesus was six or seven years old is a combined statement of the Islamic perception of Jesus's miraculous powers, of the strong child-mother bond, and of the purpose of their existence:

> While they were in Egypt, there was a good man, a dignitary, who provided for and gave to the poor. During one night when Mary and Jesus were his guests (along with others staying at his house), his money was stolen. This weighed heavily on Mary as she respected and admired his generosity. Seeing that his mother was grieved, Jesus sought from her the reason for her distress, and she told him. And then he requested the names of all the paupers who were staying there that night. Then he asked her to petition the good man to gather them all together, and this she did. And Jesus observed them, and found among them a blind man seated with an invalid upon his shoulders; and Jesus told the blind man to stand up with the invalid. The blind man

complained that he was too weak to do so. And Jesus said: 'Then how were you able to do it the other night?' Then, the blind man denied the whole matter, but the others beat him until he stood up with the invalid still upon his shoulders, and when he did so, the safety-box of the good man was discovered next to the hand of the invalid, and he being upon the blind man's shoulders. Then Jesus went to the good man, saying: 'Thus did those two plot to acquire your wealth yesterday until they managed to get it. The blind man helped with his strength, and the invalid with his eyesight'. And then the blind man admitted the truth and returned the money to the good man. He then offered half of it to Mary as a gift. And she said: 'I was not created for such things'. And he said: 'Give it, then, to your son'. She said: 'His matter is even greater than mine'.[122]

A second possible reason for the limited discussion of Mary's role as mother is its obviousness. However, for justification of this assumption, one must rely upon the histories and *qiṣaṣ* as the Qur'ān does not provide these details.[123] According to the historians, Mary's entire life after conception, with respect to routine and worldly concerns, is presented as centering around her love, guidance and protection of her son. Fearing the maliciousness of her people towards her and her son, and fearing also the wrath of Herod, she flees to unfamiliar territory, living there amongst strange people who display sometimes hostile forms of behaviour.[124] Then she returns him to his native land, equipped with full knowledge of the dangers inherent in his mission. She defends that mission while encouraging him to steadfastness. Towards the end of her life, Mary suffers the greatest pain of a human mother before she is made aware of the reality that the angels had substituted someone else for her son, Jesus, on the cross, and that Jesus had been raised up to an honoured position in Heaven.

Therefore, although Badawī, like his predecessors, devotes little space to the clarification of Mary's role as mother, he has chosen this particular characteristic to entitle his book: *The Virgin*

Mary: The Model of Compassionate Motherhood. In his commentary on Wahb ibn Munabbih's account of the above-mentioned Egyptian dignitary, who provided food and shelter for the poor, in which Mary rejects her host's reward for Jesus's having exposed the two thieves, Badawī states that during Jesus's childhood:

> He was immersed in Mary's loving compassion and affection, and received from her a righteous foundation for submission to and respect for divine worship and for meritorious works.[125]

This, together with his choice of title, indicates at least the existence of a contemporary concern amongst Muslim scholars to point out, if not emphasise, this aspect of Mary's life.

The third possibility is that since Mary was not an ordinary woman, her characteristics which resemble those of ordinary women were taken for granted, while stress was placed on her other attributes, rare amongst all human beings, whether male or female. Margaret Smith, in her explanation of the Muslim mystic's concept of the relationship between the *walī*[126] and God, deploys the following statement of the Persian mystic Shabistarī as proof that in the Muslim spiritual life there is neither male nor female:

> In God, there is no duality. In that presence I and we and thou do not exist. I and we and thou and he become one [...] The Quest and the Way and the Seeker become one.[127]

The example which Margaret Smith uses to show that this perfection of human spiritual attainment is 'found in a woman as naturally as in a man' is Mary the daughter of ʿImrān,[128] who is amongst the first group of prophets to enter Paradise.

Mary's role as mother is not de-emphasised because the role is considered unimportant in Islam; indeed, the affectionate execution of the duties of motherhood is in itself seen as a reflection of the loving mercy of God. Part of a much longer ḥadīth runs:

> Salmān reported that God's Messenger (ﷺ) said: 'Verily, on the same day that God created the heavens and the earth,

> He created one hundred parts of loving mercy [*raḥma*]. Every part of loving mercy is analogous to the space between the heavens and the earth; and out of this loving mercy He sent one part to the world, and it is from this that the mother shows affection to her child.' (Muslim)[129]

It has already been indicated that the vehicle of motherhood provides the Muslim woman with an opportunity to gain both worldly respect and Paradise.[130] But the fact remains that Mary, who was extraordinary both physically and spiritually, whose birth, sustenance and son's conception were miraculous, was a 'sign to all peoples' not only because of her perfection as a mother, but because she went beyond the ordinary in submission, devotion and purity. In other words, she was not absolved from the responsibilities of motherhood; given her status amongst God's creatures she was an ideal example of it. Nevertheless, as she was chosen to receive even higher levels of spirituality than those which are normally attainable, and as the Qur'ān itself stresses those attributes, the traditional commentators have done likewise.

CHAPTER THREE

The Symbol of Submission, the Devout, the Faithful

> O Mary! Be obedient to thy Lord, prostrate thyself and bow [as] those who bow [in worship]. (3:43)
>
> And she put faith in the words of her Lord and His scriptures, and was of the obedient. (66:12)

THE Arabic word *al-Islām* bears the sense of 'submission', that is, of the human will to the Divine. A Muslim, then, is one who submits himself to the ultimate Reality in all respects. In this sense, Mary as the image of submission is symbolic of the religion itself and furnishes an eternal theological model for all those who follow the teachings of the Qur'ān.

Mary's pre-natal dedication to worship by her mother Ḥanna was an indication, a foretoken, of the kind of life she was to lead. Ḥanna's supplication was accepted, thus making Mary the only Israelite woman to have been given this supreme honour.

> God accepted her from her mother as one consecrated to Him and made her physically beautiful, and made matters easy for her and placed her among the most pious of His slaves to learn knowledge, goodness, and His religion from them; therefore He made Zachariah her guardian so that from him she could gain this knowledge and piety.[131]

Zachariah (عليه السلام) was the spiritual guide of Mary the daughter of ʿImrān, ʿImrān being her ancestral name, representing a people whom God chose because of their religion, because they had surrendered to the Will of God, as believers in His Oneness which they celebrated through their obedience to Him.[132]

A central aspect of Mary's submission is located in her devoutness and her steadfastness in prayer. During the period from infancy to puberty when Mary led a hermit's life in her *miḥrāb*, she acquired fame for her persevering, untiring worship. The Qur'ānic attribute for Mary, *al-qunūt*, according to Ibn Kathīr means humble, pious obedience to God, and surrender to His will. Reporting the assessments of other classical scholars with respect to Mary's attribute of *al-qunūt*, Ibn Kathīr cites the early commentator Mujāhid to the effect that Mary stood in prayer until her ankles became swollen, and *al-qunūt* is 'extended prostration in prayer'. Al-ʿUzā'ī observes that she was tranquil in her *miḥrāb* kneeling, prostrating and standing until perspiration poured from her feet, and that after the angel gave her the command to obedience (3:43), she stood up in prayer until her feet hurt, flowed with blood and festered.[133] Qurṭubī, in his commentary on 66:12, notes that the plural form, *al-qānitūn*, is a description of those who worship continuously between the sunset (*maghrib*) and evening (*ʿishā'*) prayers. Ibn Abi'l-Dunyā adds that Mary performed the major ritual ablution (*ghusl*) every night.[134]

Qurṭubī's linguistic discussion of 3:43 reveals that by the phrase *maʿa ar-rākiʿīn* is meant: pray *as* they do, not *with* them, which is the interpretation favoured by many recent English translators.[135] In other words, the command is for Mary to pray alone in her *miḥrāb* as the pious among the Israelites prayed. A further linguistic analysis of 3:43 reveals that prostration (*sajda*) preceded the bowing/kneeling (*rukūʿ*) because of the connecting word 'and' (*wāw*), which makes this sequence a requirement. Qurṭubī goes on to say that the Israelite law required prostration before kneeling.[136] Zamakhsharī, however, states that perhaps it was not common in Mary's time to kneel in prayer, and that God especially commanded her to do so.[137]

In fact, material mentioned in the Talmud and other sources indicates that the usual position of prayer for the Israelites was standing and kneeling, whereas prostration was rare and confined to a previous era, taking the form of the prostration of a subject before the king in which the hands were extended and lifted up (Gen. 24:26 and Ex. 34:8), or, in the case of Elijah only (1 Kings 18:42), a form perhaps more similar to the Muslim prostration, in which he bowed to the earth with his face between his knees.[138]

In this way, one of the important images of Mary in Islam is that of the obedient servant, fully accepting her Lord's command to maintain steadfastness in prayer. Her implementation of this command included the full range of forms of prayer known to her people: standing, kneeling and the rare act of prostration. Her prayer was performed in the most intense sense. In fact, during this period of her life, she existed solely for this purpose.

Another facet of her submission is Mary's staunch sincerity of faith during the period from conception to delivery, and up until Jesus (ﷺ) speaks in the cradle, thereby redeeming her. When Mary the Virgin, who is outstanding for her chastity and piety, suddenly finds herself in an isolated place with what appears to be a handsome, young stranger, her strong faith impels her to pray to her Lord for protection. The modern Urdu writer Mawdūdī compares Mary's shock at being told by the angel that she is to bear a son with that of Zachariah, and with that of Abraham and Sarah, the latter being old, past child-bearing age (Qur'ān 28:30).[139] Although there are some obvious similarities in that conception in all these cases was miraculous, there is also the difference that Mary was young, barely an adolescent, unmarried and a female with an exalted reputation to maintain. Consequently, there must also have been an element of fear present when she questioned the angel, implying the deep incongruity of pregnancy with her lifelong purity and devoutness. Her subsequent surrender to conception, then, represents an act of total faith in the Will of her Lord and her submission to it. 'And she put faith in the power of her Lord and His Law.'[140]

A question arises, however. If Mary is the epitome of sincerity in faith, then why, when she is about to deliver, does she cry out: 'Oh, would that I had died before this, and become a thing forgotten and out of sight.'? (19:23)

Reading this plea, one is reminded perhaps of Hagar (the righteous mother of Ishmael), crying out to her Lord, alone in the desert with her child, and the subsequent miraculous appearance of Zamzam,[141] the eternal spring, just as Mary cried out and was miraculously provided with food and drink.

Mawdūdī, giving a more contemporary explication, attributes Mary's words of desperation to a 'psychologically distraught state.' He further says:

> If you think about it, you will realise that these words could not have been a result of the actual pain of childbirth, but rather a result of her intense thought about how to get through this difficult test that her Lord had placed her in, safely. How could she hide her pregnancy? And even a married woman, who experiences childbirth for the first time, suffers from anxiety, no matter how strong she is![142]

However, although it is impossible to know exactly what was going on in her mind at that moment, an extrapolation from similar cases in the Qur'ān, together with exegetic ḥadīth material, offers more conclusive answers based on a different perspective on the same events.

First of all, the classical exegetes stress the general ordinance that a Muslim must not wish for death, with reference to the following ḥadīths:

> Saʿd ibn ʿUbayd, the client of ʿAbd ar-Raḥmān ibn Azhar, narrated that the Messenger of God (ﷺ) said: 'Let none of you wish for death, for if he is a good man, he may still increase his good deeds, and if he is an evildoer, he may still desist from doing evil deeds'. (al-Bukhārī; al-Nasā'ī)[143]

Ibn Ḥajar points out that the form *lā yatamanna* strongly expresses optative negation, and that *lā yatamannayanna*, the variant form used in other narrations, even includes the grammatical inflection *nūn al-ta'kīd*, which further emphasises the absolute odiousness entailed by wishing for death.[144] Another version presents a similar conclusion:

> Abū Hurayra said: 'The Messenger of God (ﷺ) said: "Let none of you wish for death, and do not pray for it before it comes to you. Indeed, if any one of you dies, his good works are cut off, and surely, the life of a believer is not extended except for a good reason".' (Aḥmad ibn Ḥanbal)[145]

However a third more inclusive version is the key to understanding the Virgin's response:

> Anas: 'The Messenger of God (ﷺ) said: "Let none of you wish for death because of a calamity that befalls him. And if he can't help wishing, let him say: 'O God, keep me alive as long as life is better for me, and let me die if death is better for me'."' (Muslim, Bukhārī, Abū Dāwūd and Nasā'ī)[146]

In his commentary, the great Syrian scholar al-Nawawī says:

> In this ḥadīth is a clear statement about the undesirability of wishing for death because of some harm resulting from sickness, poverty, a misfortune caused by an enemy or other such calamities of this world. However, if one fears harm or temptation with regard to one's religion, it is not detestable to wish for death, according to the proper understanding of this ḥadīth.[147]

Qurṭubī explains the ḥadīth in similar terms, stating that Mary desired death in two respects, firstly that she feared she would be suspected of evil in her religion and abused, and this might tempt her to lose her assurance of faith; and secondly so that her people would not suffer because of the slander associating her with adultery, as this would be ruinous for them. Accordingly, her desire for death in this instance would entail a kind of reward, because she desired to be protected from the possibility of dying in a state of faltering faith caused by public abuse and reproach, and also she would be protecting her family from slander and possible ruin caused by their association with her.[148] The Sufi scholar Ibn 'Arabī, commenting on 19:23 states: 'There is nothing more torturing to souls than shame [ḥayā'—in the case of Mary, for the blame that would fall upon her people], to the extent that the possessor of this state wishes that he did not exist.'[149] By comparison, Qurṭubī cites the case of the prophet Joseph (عليه السلام) in which the prophet asks his Lord to end his life (12:101). Qurṭubī points out how impossible it would have been for Joseph, as an infallible prophet, to wish for death in the ordinary sense of the word, and goes on to explain that Joseph expressed this desire at the moment when he was in danger of being overcome by temptation, fearing that he might succumb to it and possibly die in a state of rebellious disbelief.[150]

This experience, in fact, was the supreme test of Mary's faith. It was such a severe test that God took mercy on her and provided her with food and drink. Having done so, He commanded her to fast, a fast which included not speaking to anyone for a day, a fast which was to replenish her faith such that she, Mary the Virgin, would be able to present to her people her newly-born child.[151]

After the birth of Jesus, Mary continued to submit willingly to whatever circumstances she was placed in by her Lord, however adverse they may have seemed. At 5:75 there is the statement: 'And his mother is a righteous woman [ṣiddīqa].' Ṭabarī states that morphologically the word ṣiddīqa is of the emphatic measure fiʿʿīl, and hence denotes extreme sincerity of faith[152] Mary is, in fact, one of the great symbols of devoutness, sincerity and submission in Islam precisely because of her absolute trust and faith in the miracles of her Lord, in addition to her belief in the message that was conveyed to her by the angel Gabriel (عليه السلام) about her conception of Jesus and his exalted purpose. Furthermore, she maintained her faith in spite of the abuse directed against her by her own people; and thus it is emphasised in 66:12 that she is a spiritual example for humanity.[153]

The important Sufi thinker Rūzbihān Baqlī sees the meaning of the passage 'and she was of the obedient' as an indication that Mary was 'steadfast, on the Straight Path in her spiritual knowledge [maʿrifa] of her Lord and her maʿrifa of her importance—as she [by submitting to God's Will] was a powerless object of scorn and derision.'[154] In another reference to Mary, Rūzbihān combines the three characteristics of submission, devotion and faithfulness in his description of her as 'sincere in your [Mary's] devotion, tenacious in your submission, meet for [Temple] service, devoted to divine destiny, and free in the place of worship with the characteristic of a loving devotee—isolated in worship from all other concerns'.[155]

Indeed, Mary's piety continues to be a symbol for Muslims of all times, partly due to the existence of her sanctuary (*miḥrāb*), which is located underground in the eastern part of the *ḥaram ash-sharīf* (the Noble Sanctuary) in Jerusalem, and is known as 'the cradle of ʿĪsā'. It is said that supplication (*duʿā'*) there is *mustaḥabb* (highly recommended), and that it is desirable to recite the Qur'ānic Chapter of Mary there and perform the *sajda*, i.e. to perform a formal, but voluntary prayer.[156] In fact, when Muslims attempt to express the esteem they have for Mary's outstanding capacity for obedience, they often become quite passionate. Badawī's comment is one such expression of this symbolic vision of Mary, the devout and the faithful:

> The heart of the Virgin Mary, together with her son, calls out to any sinner who will hear to follow the True Religion—to shed tears of repentance for that which caused him to stray from God's Cause, and calls him to humbleness and submission.[157]

CHAPTER FOUR

The Pure, the Best of Women

And when the angels said: O Mary! Lo! God hath chosen
thee and purified thee, and hath preferred thee above the
women of all nations. (3:42)

IN THEIR explication of the full meaning of the phrase
'purified thee', the classical Qur'ān scholars describe several forms
of purification: spiritual, moral and physical. Qurṭubī states that
according to Mujāhid and al-Ḥasan, the meaning is 'purified thee
from rebellious disbelief [kufr]',[158] while according to al-Zajjāj, the
'purification' is from menstruation, the blood of childbirth and
other physical impurities.[159] Khāzin mentions the physical aspect
and adds that Mary was purified from the touch of man.[160] Ṭabarī,
and also Muqātil, additionally stress Mary's (🌸) purification from
sin, from the blemishes that are found in the religion of other
women.[161] Rāzī includes the fact that she was purified from all bad
habits and from the accusations of the Jews.[162]

However, the clarification of the second part of the verse
which states that God 'hath preferred thee above the women of all
nations', aroused considerable discussion amongst the commentators. Qushayrī holds that Mary is preferred over all the women of
her time.[163] But, while Qurṭubī includes a mention of this opinion
in his exegesis, attributing it to al-Ḥasan and Ibn Jurayj, he declares

his own view to be that Mary is preferred over all women until the Day of the Sounding of the Last Trumpet, saying that this understanding is obvious from the passage, and that it is the view of Zajjāj and others.[164] Ibn Kathīr cites the statement of Ibn Abī Ḥātim that in a similar context in 21:91, the phrase *al-ʿālamīn* includes both the world of the jinn and that of the people.[165]

The reasons for this seem to be based on specific ḥadīths, the first of which is the following:

> ʿAlī narrated that he heard the Prophet (ﷺ) say: 'The best of the women of her time was Mary the daughter of ʿImrān, and the best of the women of her time is Khadīja.' (Bukhārī; Muslim; Dhahabī)[166]

Ṭabarī's personal assessment of this matter is found in his gloss on 3:43: 'Be obedient, worship and thank God for blessing, purifying and cleansing you and for preferring you to all the other women of your time.'[167] However, he includes two identical versions of the following ḥadīth with different chains of authority:

> ʿAmmār ibn Saʿd said: 'The Messenger of God (ﷺ) said: "Khadīja was preferred over the women of my community [*umma*] as Mary was preferred over the women of all nations".' (Ṭabarānī)[168]

Perhaps there is a reluctance on the part of some of the commentators to relinquish the supreme position to one of another community,[169] but the above ḥadīth and further ḥadīths indicate that the correct understanding of this verse is that Mary is preferred above all the women *of all times*:

> ʿĀ'isha asked Fāṭima: 'Did I see [you truly] when you leaned over the Messenger of God and cried; then you leaned over him and you laughed?' She said: 'He informed me that he would die from his illness, so I cried; then he informed me that I would precede the other members of his family in being reunited with him, and he said, "You are the chief lady [*sayyida*] of Paradise, with the exception of Mary the daughter of ʿImrān."' (Bukhārī; Ḥākim; Dhahabī)[170]

Dhahabī and Ibn Kathīr include another version of this ḥadīth which further affirms the priority of Mary:

> Al-Darāwardī with his chain of authorities [*isnād*] said, on the authority of Ibn ʿAbbās, 'The Messenger of God (ﷺ) said: "The chief lady of the women of Paradise after Mary is Fāṭima, and Khadīja, and the wife of the Pharaoh, Āsiya".' (Dhahabī; Ibn ʿAsākir)[171]

In the version of Ibn ʿAsākir, instead of the copula *wāw* ('and'), Ibn ʿAbbās is quoted as having said *thumma* (implying a sequence: *then Khadīja, then* Āsiya), upon which Ibn Kathīr concludes that Mary's status as the most preferred of Paradise is *ṣaḥḥ al-ʿayn* (the soundest choice). He thus ranks the four as follows: firstly, Mary the daughter of ʿImrān, secondly Fāṭima, thirdly Khadīja and fourthly Āsiya.[172] Ibn Kathīr then concedes that 'Indeed, God purified and preferred Mary above the women of the world of her time, and it is possible that her preference was above all women.'[173] He buttresses his conclusion with the following ḥadīth:

> The Messenger of God (ﷺ) said, 'God married me in Paradise to Mary the daughter of ʿImrān and to the wife of the Pharaoh and the sister of Moses.' (Ṭabarānī)[174]

Then Ibn Kathīr discusses some rejected ḥadīths, one of which is attributed to Ibn ʿAsākir on the authority of Ibn ʿUmar. Ibn Kathīr states that the first part of the ḥadīth in which the angel Gabriel greets Khadīja at the time of her illness and informs her of a house in Paradise is *ṣaḥīḥ* (sound), but the subsequent text which defines the nature of the house and places it between the houses of Mary and Āsiya is extremely *gharīb* (strange) and is supported by an obscure chain of authorities. He further mentions various versions of a ḥadīth about Mary and Āsiya compiled by Ibn ʿAsākir and Abū Zūrʿak, in which it is said that the rock in the Mosque of the Dome of the Rock in the Noble Sanctuary of Jerusalem is on top of a palm tree, which is on one of the rivers of Paradise, and under the palm tree are Mary the daughter of ʿImrān and Āsiya the daughter of Muzāḥim stringing the pearls of the inhabitants of Paradise until the day of Resurrection.[175] Although in a symbolic sense the intention behind this account may perhaps be seen as an allegorical description of the great spirituality of both Mary and Āsiya, to the purely exoteric scholar it falls in the category of storytelling, and is rejected by Dhahabī as 'an obvious lie.'[176] Ibn Kathīr, who bases his commentary primarily on ḥadīth, states:

> This ḥadīth is rejected [*munkar*] and forged [*mawḍūʿ*]. Those versions of ḥadīth compiled by Ibn ʿAsākir and transmitted by Kaʿb al-Aḥbār, were obtained from Isrā'īlī sources,[177] among which is that which is not true, is fabricated and recorded by unbelievers or the ignorant, and this ḥadīth is of that category. And God knows best [what the truth of the matter is].[178]

Such disputed ḥadīths are, however, not necessary in making a case for Mary's status, as the Qur'ānic text and numerous sound ḥadīths indicate that the four most outstanding women are Mary, then Khadīja, Fāṭima and Āsiya, although not necessarily in that order.[179] Moreover, Mary is the most outstanding woman of all nations of all times and places, as certified by the Qur'ān itself—and she and Āsiya are the only two women named in the Qur'ān—while Khadīja and Fāṭima showed excellence above all women of their time and will be rewarded as such in Paradise.

In Islam, Mary's chastity is unquestioned. The Qur'ān clearly states:

> And she who was chaste . . . (21:91)

> She said: How can I have a son when no mortal hath touched me, neither have I been unchaste? (19:20)

Ṭabarī paraphrases the meaning of 19:20 thus: 'When no mortal has touched me, either from the point of view of *ḥalāl* [allowed acts] or *ḥarām* [forbidden acts].'[180] Thus, because of Mary's purity of body and soul, she is entitled *al-batūl*. She is called the Virgin Mary in the Christian context, thus stressing the physical aspect of her purity, but the Arabic word, *al-batūl* implies more, as the scholars have noted.

According to the classical dictionary *Lisān al-ʿArab*, the root of *batūl*, *b.t.l*, has the sense of 'severance', and the original meaning of the words *batūl*, *batīl*, and *batīla* is: a palm shoot which has separated itself from its mother tree. The verb which is related to the form *batūl* is *tabattala*, and the phrase *tabattala ilā Allāh* means to withdraw or to cut oneself off in order to devote oneself sincerely to divine worship. Thus, if God's servant severs all concerns and devotes himself totally to His worship, he has *tabattala*, i.e., has separated himself from everything except the cause of God and obedience to Him.[181] *Lisān al-ʿArab* further states that 'the *batūl* among the women' is the woman who separates herself from men, having no desire or need for them. Thus, Mary the Virgin [*al-ʿadhrāʾ*] was called the *batūl* because of her abstention from marriage and her severance from all worldly preoccupations in order to worship God.[182] *Batūl* may also refer to physical beauty, in addition to spiritual excellence; consequently, al-Khāzin describes Mary as the most beautiful and the most excellent of women of her time.[183]

Mary's characteristics of spiritual and bodily purity are reiterated in the various stories and accounts of her life, one of which is found in Wahb ibn Munabbih's tale about Joseph the Carpenter's awareness of her pregnancy, which at first he found to be unacceptably bizarre: 'Then he considered what he knew about her religiousness and her worship,' at which point he realised that the situation was beyond his ken.[184] Another account found in the *Faḍāʾil* literature[185] portrays Mary's physical purity:

> Saʿīd ibn ʿAbd al-ʿAzīz said: 'In the time of the Israelites there was a spring [or well] in Jerusalem around the site of the Spring of Silwān. If a woman was accused of adultery or fornication, she would drink from this spring. If she were innocent no harm would come to her, but if she were guilty, she would die. So when Mary became pregnant, they brought her there. She drank from it, and nothing happened except good. And she prayed to God not to let her be dishonoured as she was a believing woman, and the spring dried up.' (al-Khaṭīb)[186]

From the perspective both of the customary practices of the Jews at the time of Mary's birth, and of those presented in the Qur'ān and Sunna, Mary's dedication to worship and her conscious abstention from marriage are characteristics which set her apart from the ordinary. For Jewish believers, such dedication had previously been reserved for men, and did not entail lifelong abstention from marriage. And as the following discussion indicates, the fact that Mary was chosen to possess these characteristics is an even greater distinguishing factor in the Islamic context, as it places her outside the realm of what is generally advised for the believers, male or female.

The first factor to be considered is 'purity from the touch of man' (3:47 and 19:20). In Islam, the injunction for the Muslim is to be morally chaste before marriage; then to marry if possible, then preserving this chastity in the sense of abstaining from extramarital relations:

> For men and women who guard their chastity [. . .] for such has God prepared forgiveness and great reward. (33:35)

> Let those who find not the wherewithal for marriage keep themselves chaste until God gives them means [. . .] (24:33)

As implied in 24:33, and as stated in the following ḥadīth, marriage is the desirable state for the Muslim, as it provides a protection from sin:

> ʿAbdullāh [ibn Masʿūd] said: 'The Messenger of God (ﷺ) said to us, "O you young men, whoever amongst you has the means, let him marry because it is the best aid to modesty [sc. the best restrainer of the eye from looking at which should not be seen], and the best protection from fornication. And whoever cannot afford to marry, then fasting is required from him, as it is a means of cleansing."' (Bukhārī and Muslim)[187]

The Qur'ānic injunctions at 33:35 and 24:33 apply to both men and women; thus Muslim women are normally expected to marry, and to remarry in case of widowhood or divorce.[188] An exception to this condition is found in the special status of the widows of the Prophet (ﷺ), who were prohibited from marrying after his death:

> Nor is it right for you that ye should annoy the Messenger of God, or that you should ever marry his widows after him. (33:53)

Another exception is the Blessed Virgin, who was designated never to marry, to remain together with her son, as a 'sign for [all] peoples'. (21:91)

The second consideration is the Islamic perspective on total devotion to worship. The practice of separating oneself from worldly concerns for limited periods of time for the purpose of spiritual worship is fully accepted as an act of Sunna:

> ʿĀ'isha said that the Prophet (ﷺ) used to go into retreat [*iʿtikāf*] during the last ten days of every Ramaḍān until he died; then, his wives practiced *iʿtikāf* after his death. (Bukhārī and Muslim)[189]

The Muslim is hence encouraged to go beyond the fulfillment of his obligatory worship. According to the following ḥadīths, however, he or she should not carry this to the extent of totally neglecting wordly responsibilities:

> On the authority of Anas, a group of the Companions of the Prophet (ﷺ) asked the wives of the Prophet (ﷺ) about his conduct in private. And some of them [the Companions] said: 'I will not marry women', and some of them said: 'I will not sleep on bedding'. So the Prophet (ﷺ) praised God and glorified Him, and said: 'What is on the minds of these people? They have said this and that, but I pray and sleep, fast and break my fast, and marry women. And whoever wishes to reject my example [*sunna*] is not one of mine' [i.e. not part of the Community of Islam]. (Muslim and Aḥmad ibn Ḥanbal)[190]

> Saʿd ibn Abī Waqqās said: "Uthmān ibn Maẓʿūn wanted to live a monklike existence [*yātabattal*], and the Messenger of God (ﷺ) forbade him [from doing so], and if he had

allowed him to do so, we would have castrated ourselves.' (Muslim)[191]

The last of the two ḥadīths emphasise the importance of choosing a path of moderation, in spite of the fact that it may be difficult for the fervent believer who wants to abandon him or herself to total worship, ignoring marriage and other worldly attachments. But Mary, the universal symbol of female purity and piety, was permitted to do what was forbidden to others.

The final argument for the special status of Mary's purity is found in Ibn al-Qayyim's exegesis of the Qur'ānic chapter of al-Taḥrīm. He begins his commentary on this point with verses 10–12:

> God citeth an example for those who disbelieve: the wife of Noah and the wife of Lot, who were under two of Our righteous slaves yet betrayed them so that they [the husbands] availed them naught against God. And it was said: Enter the Fire along with those who enter. (66:10)
>
> And God citeth an example for those who believe: the wife of Pharaoh when she said: 'My Lord! Build for me a home with Thee in the Garden, and deliver me from Pharaoh and his doings, and deliver me from the people who work evil.' (66:11)
>
> And Mary the daughter of ʿImrān, who preserved her chastity. We breathed therein something of Our Spirit. And she put faith in the words of her Lord and His scriptures, and was of the obedient. (66:12)

Ibn al-Qayyim then offers an interesting discussion of the above texts:

> Thus three kinds of women are mentioned. Firstly, the unbelieving woman who had a close relationship with a pious man; secondly, the pious woman who had a close relationship with an unbelieving man; and thirdly, the celibate woman who had no relationship with any man; that is, who had no husband, neither believer nor unbeliever. And there is wonderful knowledge in these examples [66:10–12].

> There is an explication which conforms to the style of the Sūra.[192] These three verses allude to the mention of the wives of the Prophet (ﷺ), and are a warning to them about acts which they did which could have been used against him,[193] a warning that if they do not obey God and His Messenger (ﷺ) and seek the Hereafter, their association with the Messenger of God (ﷺ) will be of no avail, just as it did not avail the wives of Noah and of Lot.[194]

Ibn al-Qayyim then cites Yaḥyā ibn Salām's statement that God gave the first example of the wives of Noah and Lot as a warning to the Prophet's (ﷺ) wives ʿĀ'isha and Ḥafsa; then He gave the second example of Āsiya to encourage them to dutiful steadfastness.[195] Ibn al-Qayyim concludes his argument with the following statement:

> And in the citing of Mary as an example for the believers, there is also another point, which is that from God's perspective there is no blemish on her. God's enemies accused her of fornication, attributing to her that which God had liberated her from, by His creating her to be the supreme example of the most righteous [*al-ṣiddīqa al-kubrā*],[196] the most preferred [*al-muṣṭafā*][197] of the women of all nations.[198]

A factor which buttresses Ibn al-Qayyim's connection of the first twelve verses of al-Taḥrīm is the underlying awareness that the three women, ʿĀ'isha, Ḥafṣa and Mary, had been falsely accused, and subsequently vindicated. Qurṭubī draws a similar parallel in his commentary on 24:4:

> And those who accuse chaste, honourable women, but bring not four witnesses, flog them with eighty stripes and never afterwards accept their testimony. They are evildoers. (24:4)

He says that although some say this verse was revealed for the case of ʿĀ'isha, others say it was revealed for women in general who were falsely accused; and the prime example he gives is Mary and the accusation against her: 'O sister of Aaron [. . .]' (19:28)[199]

Mary's preference over other outstanding women appears in a number of ḥadīths, some of which have already been cited. It also appears in the context of a conversation with the Prophet's companion Ibn Ṣafwān, in which ʿĀ'isha extols Mary and cites verses which were revealed about her, alluding to the episode of the false accusations:

> ʿAbd ar-Raḥmān ibn al-Ḍaḥḥāk said: "Abdullāh ibn Ṣafwān informed him that he went to ʿĀ'isha and she said: "I have received about nine blessed experiences, which no [woman] has had, excepting what God vouchsafed to Mary (☙). By God, I am not saying this to boast over my companions." So Ibn Ṣafwān enquired, "And what are they?" She replied, "The angel came to the Messenger of God with my image; and he [the Prophet] married me as a virgin; and he received revelation while we were retired together; and I was among the most beloved of people to him; and verses were revealed about me as the Muslim community [*umma*] was about to be destroyed; and I saw Gabriel, and none of his other wives saw him except me; and he was buried in my house, and no-one was close to him—except the angels—but me".'[200]

Finally, the following ḥadīth sheds further light on Mary's supreme postion. It warns the believers not to neglect the importance of four women. Mary, being the first mentioned, is by implication given the highest status:

> Anas ibn Mālik said: 'The Prophet (☙) said, 'Reckon with the oustanding women of all nations: Mary, and Khadīja, and Āsiya the daughter of Muzāḥim, and Fāṭima the daughter of Muḥammad.' (Tirmidhī and Dhahabī)[201]

In response to this ḥadīth and Qur'ān 3:42, Rāzī deduces:`

> that these four women are preferred above other women, while the verse indicates that Mary is preferred above *all* women. And statements of those who limit this preference for her to the world of her time only have missed the obvious meaning [of the passage].[202]

Qurṭubī summarises his assessment of this aspect of Mary's characteristics in similar terms: 'The obvious sense of the Qur'ān and ḥadīth demands the conclusion that Mary is the most preferred woman of all the world, from Eve to the last woman on earth at the Final Hour.'[203] Focussing on her interior purity, Rūzbihān Baqlī in his commentary on 21:91 describes Mary's constancy in worship, her saintliness, and the purity of her soul (*nafs*).[204]

Thus the evidence of the Qur'ān and ḥadīth indicates that while Khadīja or Fāṭima may be considered the best of women of her time, Mary, peace be upon her, is the best woman of all times. She is the physically and spiritually pure, and conclusively singled out as a sign for all peoples (21:91). Mary's purity is, in fact, one of her key characteristics. It is this dimension of her being that made her a possible receptacle for the miraculous conception. And in the purity of her spiritual striving is found a symbolic goal for others, awakening them to a pristine vision of the meaning of obedience, devoutness and worship, the inner reality for the believer.

CHAPTER FIVE

The Sincere, the Righteous:
Saint or Prophetess?

And his mother was a truthful, righteous woman [siddīqa].[205] (5:75)

THE following account describes Mary (☝), as a spiritual light comparable to the prophets:

Al-Walīd ibn Muslim related: 'Some of our respected elders [ashyākh] narrated that when the Messenger of God (☝) appeared at the Noble Sanctuary of Bayt al-Maqdis on the night of the Isrā',[206] two radiant lights were shining to the right of the mosque and to the left, so he asked, "O Gabriel! What are those two lights?" And he replied, "The one on your right is the [miḥrāb] of your brother David, and the one on your left is the grave of your sister Mary".'[207]

This 'luminous' attribute of the Marian phenomenon points up the question of what Mary's precise *theological* status is in Islam. This issue essentially forms a culmination of the dispute documented in the previous chapter, over whether she was the best woman of her time, or of all time. The discussion now broadens to address Mary's hierarchical status amid the totality of all God's creatures. Is she to be considered as the righteous (the ṣiddīqa), only, or as a saintly, holy woman (a *waliyya*),[208] or prophetess as well? To most of the classical Qur'ān commentators, the question of whether or not Mary should be ranked among the prophets was extremely important. Two basic themes recur in their discussions. One is the theoretical issue of whether or not any woman can in principle be classified amongst the prophets, and the other takes the form of a parallel question as to whether Mary, specifically, should be classed as a *waliyya* or a prophetess. Here there is a marked lack of consensus, stemming from the fact that although Mary's case is mentioned in the Qur'ānic chapter *al-Anbiyā'* (The Prophets) along with others who are more uncontroversially designated as prophets, she is not explicitly named as such; nor is she actually called a prophet (*nabiyya*), anywhere else in the Qur'ān. This being the case, while the Qur'ān does state that some of the prophets were also 'messengers' (*rusul*) and mentions others as 'prophets' (*anbiyā'*) only,[209] the possibility remains of a classification of 'prophet' existing separately from that of 'messenger'. Some human beings may have been designated as 'messenger' and 'prophet', and others as 'prophet' only; and in view of this, the commentators have surveyed the evidence with respect to Mary and drawn their various conclusions.[210]

Although some of the traditional Sunni scholars concede that there exist some theologians who attribute prophethood to Mary and other women, they still prefer the opinion that saintly women in general are to be formally classified as *ṣiddīqāt*.[211] Bayḍāwī, in his commentary on 3:42, accepts the opinion of those who deny that the Qur'ānic statement that Mary is preferred above the women of all nations points to her prophethood, claiming that this is a conclusion accepted by the consensus (*ijmā*ʿ) of the scholars.[212] He locates the basis of this denial in the phrase *mā arsalnā min qablika illā rijāl*, which is found in 12:109, 16:43 and 21:17.[213] For instance:

> And *We sent not before thee* [*any messenger*] *save men* whom We inspired from among the folk of the townships. Have they not travelled in the land and seen how was the end of

> those who went before them? And verily, the abode of the Hereafter, for those who ward off [evil], is best. Have ye then no sense? (12:109)

Basing the argument against Mary's prophethood on this text firstly presumes the absence of a distinction between prophet and messenger, as the reference here is to messengers only. Secondly it distorts the meaning of the text, as the phrase is taken out of context in order to stress the word *rijāl* (men), while it seems just as likely that the intention is to emphasise that the messengers were normal human beings whom God inspired, rather than some other form of creature, such as angels.[214] Thirdly, it implies that *rijāl* solely covers human beings of masculine gender, whereas the masculine form in Arabic, as in English, can be used inclusively to denote all human beings. The ḥadīth referred to in chapter two about the mother who shared the one date with her two daughters is one such example, in which the masculine pronoun *hu* (him) clearly includes the mother who is the focus of the ḥadīth. Thus, although none of the traditional scholars would accept the premise that Mary was a messenger, as there is no evidence for this, the denial of her *prophethood* based on the argument of Bayḍāwī and others with respect to 'and We sent not before thee [any messenger] save men' (*mā arsalnā min qablika illā rijāl*), is unpersuasive.

Another factor which weakens the position of those who reject Mary's prophetic status is their apparent hesitance to accord such a position of greatness to women outside their own faith-community (*umma*). This is seen in their deployment of the following ḥadīth as proof that Mary was not above Khadīja and Fāṭima, thus implying that since neither of them were prophetesses, neither was Mary.[215]

> Abū Hurayra said: 'I heard the Messenger of God (ﷺ) saying, "The women of Quraysh[216] are the best of those who ride camels, and the most loving to children, and the best guardians of their husbands' property".' Abū Hurayra added, 'And Mary the daughter of 'Imrān never rode a camel.' (Bukhārī)[217]

To buttress his point, Ṭabarī includes an additional statement suggesting that if the Prophet (ﷺ) had known that Mary had ridden a camel, then he would not have preferred anyone above her.[218] Ibn Ḥajar, however, deepens the understanding of the ḥadīth by pointing out that Abū Hurayra's statement indicates that the discussion is only about Arabs, referring to the special preference within that stated group for Khadīja, Fāṭima, ʿĀʾisha, and others. And he adds that if it is certain that women may become prophets, then Mary obviously stands outside this discourse entirely because there is no human distinction above the rank of prophethood; therefore, this particular reference is intended for Arab women only and was not intended to include other saintly women. In other words:

> Abū Hurayra meant by his statement that Mary did not enter into the discussion of these women mentioned with reference to good characteristics because the reference was directed only to those who rode camels, and Mary was not among those who rode camels, and because he was of the view that Mary was the most excellent [most preferred] among all women.[219]

Ibn Kathīr summarises the arguments put forward by those who reject the possibility of Marian prophecy. His commentary suggests an inconclusive determination on his own part as to whether or not Mary should be considered a prophetess. However the following discussion suggests that he personally accepts the possibility that she might be considered as such, but is unwilling to disagree openly with what he considers to be the prevalent opinion. Ibn Kathīr's commentary on 3:42 in his *Qiṣaṣ* does not follow his usual logical exegesis based on sound ḥadīth. He begins by stating that it is possible that Mary is preferred over all the women of her time. As evidence, he cites the phrase *innī'ṣṭafaytuka ʿalā'n-nās* found in 7:144:

> [God] said: 'O Moses! I have chosen [preferred] thee above [other] men by My speaking [unto thee]. So take that which I have given to thee, and be among the thankful.' [7:144]

Ibn Kathīr, discussing the phrase out of context, states that it is known that Abraham (عليه السلام) is preferred above Moses (عليه السلام) and that

Muḥammad (ﷺ) is preferred over both of them, in spite of this phrase which appears to indicate the contrary.[220] However, in its context, the phrase seems to refer to the specific acts mentioned, the specific message which Moses was given, and the fact that God did obviously prefer Moses by speaking to him without the intermediary of an angel. The statement in the verse does not appear to be a general assessment or comparative classification of those preferred by God, whereas the reference to Mary comes at the end of 3:42 and refers back to the entire verse, thus apparently making a definitive statement about Mary's preference and purity, with respect to all women.

Ibn Kathīr further bases this opinion on the text *wa-l laqad ikhtarnāhum ʿalā ʿilmin ʿalā al-ʿālamīn:*[221]

And We chose them above the nations, knowingly. [44:32]

He says that although the expression 'above the nations' appears in the verse, it is not proof of Israelite supremacy, 'as the community of Islam is preferred over all previous communities, is larger in number, and so on.'[222] Perhaps, due to his own personal preference for his own community, Ibn Kathīr seems to have obscured the basic point of 44:32, as this text is intrinsically connected to the previous ones and to the subsequent one by the copula *wāw* ('and'). Thus the sense of the full statement is that the Israelites were delivered from Pharaoh, the tyrant and transgressor, and chosen above the nations, and granted signs as a trial.[223] The apparent conclusion is that God's preference for the Israelites is indicated by His having sent so many prophets to them, and thus having given them so many opportunities for guidance and for Paradise.[224] There is no apparent indication that they were preferred as the best, or the largest, or the most intelligent community (the point which Ibn Kathīr is arguing against), while in the case of Mary, the criterion for the general preference is stated in the same text 3:42.

Ibn Kathīr then states that on the other hand it is possible that the understanding of 3:42 is that there is a preference 'in general' for Mary above the women of the world, of those who preceded her or came after her, as there is no other Qur'ānic statement which opposes this text.[225] He concludes his discussion in his *Tales of the Prophets* by recording that the view of the majority of 'the people of tradition and scholarly consensus' (*ahl as-sunna wa al-jamāʿa*), according to Abū'l-Ḥasan al-Ashʿarī,[226] is that based on 5:75. Mary is the *ṣiddīqa*, and there is no objection to her being the most preferred of all the well-known righteous women, those who preceeded her and those who came after her.[227] However, in his remarks on 5:75 in his *Commentary*, although he reiterates the argument concerning 'and We sent not before thee [any messenger] save men' and uses it to buttress his statement that 5:75 is an indication that Mary was not a prophetess, but was a sincere believer in God and that this was the highest of her saintly attributes, he admits that Mary and other women did receive revelation through the angel, and that this is in fact the meaning of prophecy, although he adds that the majority believe that God sent only men as prophets.[228]

Some other commentators fully accept the classification of Mary as a prophetess. Their argument rests primarily on an explication of 3:42 based on two sound ḥadīths and an understanding of the meaning of prophethood/prophecy (*nubuwwa*) which includes relevant Qur'ānic passages about women and revelation. The following are two related versions of the first of the two ḥadīths on which they base their conclusions:

> Abū Hurayra narrated that the Messenger of God (ﷺ) said: 'Each person, when his mother gives birth to him, has an innate disposition to the Truth [*ʿalā al-fiṭra*];[229] and it is only his parents who later make him a Jew or a Christian or a Zoroastrian; and if his parents are Muslims, then he will be a Muslim. Each person when his mother gives birth to him is struck by Satan in his sides, except Mary and her son.' (Muslim)[230]

> Abū Hurayra narrated that the Messenger of God (ﷺ) said: 'There is no child who is born without the prod of Satan, from which he begins to cry, except the son of Mary and his mother.' Then Abū Hurayra said: 'Recite if you wish, "I crave Thy protection for her and her offspring from Satan

the outcast".' (Bukhārī; Muslim; Aḥmad ibn Ḥanbal; Ṭabarī; al-Ḥākim; Ibn Khuzayma)[231]

The first ḥadīth stresses the Islamic doctrinal point that everyone is born pure of sin, but that Satan immediately interferes, except in the case of Mary and Jesus (ﷺ), and also that it is one's environment and upbringing that either maintain one's purity or distort it. Qurṭubī quotes the traditional scholars as saying that '[The second version] informs us that God answered the prayer [*duʿā'*] of Mary's mother. Thus it is that Satan prods all the children of Adam, even the prophets and saints, except Mary and her son.[232] By 'prodding' is meant that Satan strives to seduce every individual by influencing him, except Mary and her son Jesus;[233] thus they were not afflicted by sin, as all other human beings are.[234]

The question may arise as to why Mary, who was born to be eternally free of sin, devoted herself so staunchly to worship. One answer may be found in 3:43. In other words, Mary's worship was an indication of her full submission to her Lord's command of obedience. Another answer is found by comparison with the Prophet Muḥammad's (ﷺ) response to a similar question under similar circumstances:

> Al-Mughīra ibn Shuʿba said: 'The Prophet (ﷺ) prayed until his feet became swollen; and he was asked, "Do you burden yourself with this when God has pardoned you for what preceded of your sins and what is to come?" But he replied, "Should I not be a grateful servant?"' (Muslim)[235]

Mary's intense worship indicates both her desire to fulfill her Lord's command, and her gratefulness for having been chosen for her unique position above the women of the world.

The following ḥadīth represents the second basic argument for Mary's status as prophetess:

> Abū Mūsā narrated that the Messenger of God (ﷺ) said: 'Among men, there are many who have been perfect [as human beings], but among women, none have been perfect except for Mary the daughter of ʿImrān and Āsiya, the wife

of the Pharaoh. And the excellence of ʿĀ'isha over other women is like the excellence of broth [*tharīd*] over all other foods.' (Bukhārī and Muslim)[236]

Even those who do not attribute prophethood to Mary admit that this ḥadīth places her in the highest category, and therefore their discussions tend to be governed by seemingly extraneous factors, such as the apparent lack of willingness on their part to give such high status to one outside their own community (*umma*). An example of this perspective in response to this particular ḥadīth is Nawawī's commentary, in which he concurs with the Qāḍī ʿIyāḍ's assessment:

> This ḥadīth is proof to those who acclaim the prophethood of women, and of Āsiya and Mary; but the majority are of the opinion that the two are not prophets, but two righteous and saintly women who were *awliyā'*. And the meaning of *kāmila* [perfect] here is: the utmost of all virtues, including the qualities of reverence and worship. The Qāḍī ʿIyāḍ further states that if we say they are two prophetesses, then there is no question that other women do not come close to them, but if we say they are two saintly women, then there is no objection to indicating others similar to them in this *umma*.[237]

Ibn Kathīr arrives at a similar although less decisive conclusion when he suggests that the 'perfection' of Mary (﷌) and Āsiya perhaps refers to the fact that they were the only two women who were protectors and guardians of prophets (Moses and Jesus), although this does not deny the 'perfection' of others 'in this community'; then he proceeds to praise Khadīja, Fāṭima and ʿĀ'isha highly, in what appears to be an attempt to compensate for the fact that Mary and Āsiya have been singled out above these other outstanding women.[238] However, throughout his discussion he consistently uses the phrase ʿalayhā as-salām (peace be upon her) for Mary, a phrase which customarily represents a prayer for a prophet,[239] while he uses the phrase *raḍiya'llāhu ʿanhā* (may God be pleased with her) for the other highly respected women, Khadīja, Fāṭima and Ā'isha, a prayer which Muslims say for the Companions of the Prophet Muḥammad (ﷺ). Ibn Kathīr thus indicates his awareness of a greater distinction than he is willing to admit conclusively.

Qurṭubī strongly favours the opinion of those who accept female prophethood, especially Mary. In his explication of 3:42: 'purified and chose thee', he includes the ḥadīth under discussion and states:

> Our scholars [*ʿulamā'*][240] have said that 'perfection' [*kamāl*] is the highest degree for a human being and the most complete, as absolute Perfection is attributed only to God, the Most High. And there is no doubt that the most perfect type of human beings are prophets, then the holy ones among the pious and the martyrs and the righteous.[241]

Consequently, it has been said that the *kamāl* mentioned in this ḥadīth means *nubuuwa* (prophethood). Thus the indication here is clearly that Mary and Āsiya were prophets, 'peace be upon them both.'[242] Throughout his exegesis of the texts which refer to Mary, Qurṭubī mentions two factors which he believes confirm Mary's status as prophetess: firstly 3:45, in which she receives revelation by means of an angel as occurred to all other prophets; and secondly 21:91, which records that she was made a 'sign' as a clear proof of God's miraculous power.[243] Qurṭubī rejects the argument of those who say that in Mary's encounter with the Archangel (عليه السلام) at the time of the annunciation it was as if she had a conversation, rather than revelation, because Gabriel appeared to her in the image of a man.[244] Indeed, the Qur'ān itself makes it clear that Mary's acceptance of the angel's message was dependent on her acceptance of the fact that he brought the message to her from her Lord. Moreover, Gabriel states *God's* message to her in 19:21.[245] Qurṭubī further states that it is possible for Mary to have been righteous (*ṣiddīqa*) and at the same time a prophetess, as in the case of the prophet Idrīs (عليه السلام).[246]

> And make mention in the Book, of Idrīs. Lo! He was a truthful, righteous man [*ṣiddīq*], a Prophet. [19:56]

Similarly, Ibn Ḥajar al-ʿAsqalānī concludes that the ḥadīth which speaks of *kamāl* clearly indicates that there is something different about Mary and Āsiya, and that this difference could not be simply that they are saints. because many other women fit into that category; therefore, it must be that they are genuine recipients of prophecy. He states that this is indicated by the fact that the ḥadīth limits this category of 'perfection' amongst women to these two only. Then, making an argument based on the same premise as that of Qurṭubī, he states:

> The most perfect type of human beings are prophets, followed by the *awliyā'* and the *ṣiddīqūn* [righteous] and the *shuhadā'* [martyrs]. And if they [Mary and Āsiya] are not to be considered prophetesses, then there is no reason to consider that there exists among women a single saint [*waliyya*], or a righteous one [*ṣiddīqa*], or a martyr [*shahīda*]. Yet the reality is that these characteristics are frequently met with amongst women.[247]

Ibn Ḥajar includes al-Ḥasan al-Baṣrī among the rejectors of Marian prophecy, but quotes Subkī as stating that none of the rejectors' arguments are sound.[248] Ibn Ḥajar further states that the purport of 3:42 is that God indicates that Mary was a prophetess, although this is not directly stated, and he then summarises a discussion put forth by the Cordovan scholar Ibn Ḥazm in support of this conclusion.[249]

In his work *al-Fiṣal*, Ibn Ḥazm presents the most inclusive argument in favour of prophethood for women. His discussion is logical and cohesive, and is based primarily on his rational understanding of the relevant Qur'ānic texts. He begins by mentioning that disagreement had arisen in Cordova, where a few scholars had begun to reject the concept of prophethood amongst women, based on: 'And We sent not before thee [any messengers] save men.' But, he says:

> In fact there is no disagreement over this point, as the discussion does not concern God sending women as messengers, it

> concerns prophethood without a Message. Therefore the seeker of the truth in this question must look at the expression 'prophethood'/prophecy [*nubuwwa*], in the language in which God spoke to us. And we will find that this expression originates from *inbā'*, which is 'granting perception', and any person to whom God, the Most Great and the Most High, gives prior perception of what is to come, or reveals to him a message for him to do something with God's command, is a prophet, without doubt.[250]

Then Ibn Ḥazm provides examples of what revelation is *not*:

> And this does not refer to 'inspiration' [*ilhām*] which is instinctive [*ṭabīʿa*], like the statement of God: 'And thy Lord inspired [*awḥā*] the bees to build habitations in the hills . . . ' [16:68]. Nor does it refer to 'assuming' [*ẓann*], and 'imagination' [*tawahhum*], about which there is no certainty of truth except to a madman. Nor does it refer to *kahāna* ['predicting', 'fortune-telling'], which comes from eavesdropping on the devils, who cast off a lighted match, and about which God says: 'Likewise We have appointed unto every prophet an enemy—devils of men and *jinn* who inspire [*yūḥī*] one another with flowery speech deceptively'. [6:112] Nor does it refer to 'astrology' which is an attempt at knowledge. Nor does it refer to a dream 'vision' [*ru'yā*] whose status as true or false is not known.[251]

Ibn Ḥazm then provides examples of what prophetic revelation *is*. He explains that the revelation (*waḥy*) which is prophecy (*nubuwwa*) consists of a message which comes from God in order to inform the recipient of something. God appraises this person of the truth of the Message and its origin by means of an inner intuitive sight about which there is no doubt, or by sending the angel to him with the Message.[252]

Ibn Ḥazm then proceeds to detail his argument in support of female prophecy, with especial reference to Mary. Basing his discussion on the above definition of *nubuwwa*, he affirms that the Qur'ān states that God has sent angels to women, and that He has furnished them with information via revelation of His truth. For example, the angels gave the good news of the coming of Isaac (ﷺ) to his mother:

> And his wife was standing [there], and she laughed, then We gave her good tidings [*bashsharnāhā*] [of the birth] of Isaac; and [after him], of Jacob. (11:71)
>
> They said: 'Dost thou wonder at the commandment of God?' (11:73)

Ibn Ḥazm implies that Sarah is thus logically understood to be a prophetess, as it is unreasonable to consider that speech from an angel could be to anyone but a prophet. He also gives the example of the mother of Moses, when God commanded her through *waḥy* to cast her son in the river, promising her that her son would return to her, and that He would make him a prophet and a messenger:

> And We inspired [revealed to—*awḥaynā*] the mother of Moses, saying: 'Suckle him, and when you fear for him, then cast him into the river and fear not nor grieve. Lo! We shall bring him back unto thee and shall make him [one] of Our messengers.' (28:7)[253]

Asserting that this is prophecy without doubt, Ibn Ḥazm explains that if she had not trusted the prophecy from God to her, she would not have cast her son into the river because if she had done so as a result of a vision or a feeling, it would have been an act of madness. Ibn Ḥazm compares her experience of revelation to cast her son into the river with that of Abraham (ﷺ) to sacrifice his son:

> And when [his son] was old enough to walk with him, [Abraham] said: 'O my son! I have seen in a dream that I must sacrifice thee. So look, what thinkest thou?' He said: 'O my father! Do as thou art commanded. God willing, thou shalt find me of the steadfast in patience.' (37:102)
>
> Then, when they had both surrendered [to God], and he had flung him down on his forehead, We called unto him: 'O Abraham! Thou hast already fulfilled the vision [*ru'yā*]. Lo! thus do We reward the good.' (37:103–5)

Ibn Ḥazm considers that if the prophet Abraham had done so following intuition, without ascertainment from his Lord (*nubuwwa*), it would have been madness, and such would have been unworthy of so great a man.

Ibn Ḥazm considers Mary to be unquestionably a prophetess. He states that God sent the angel Gabriel (ﷺ) to Mary with a message to her (19:19), which he describes as 'genuine prophecy' (*nubuwwa ṣaḥīḥa*). In addition, he refers to other miraculous experiences, such as the divine provisions in the *miḥrāb*. Ibn Ḥazm then places Mary in the general category of prophets by applying the statement in 19:58 to the Chapter of Mary as a whole:

> Those were they among the prophets to whom God showed favour . . . [19:58]

He points out that Mary (ﷺ) is mentioned among those prophets in the Chapter of Mary, and this inclusion of her within the general category of prophets renders it impossible to make an exception and exclude her from that category. He further states that neither does the Qur'ānic statement 'And his mother was a righteous woman' (*ṣiddīqa*) (5:75) rule out her being a prophetess, as elsewhere the Qur'ān, in connection with the prophet Joseph (ﷺ) says: 'Joseph! O thou truthful [upright] one' (*ṣiddīq*) (12:46), which does not impugn his prophetic status.

Then he mentions the ḥadīth *kamula min ar-rijāl*,[254] in which he indicates that the Prophet (ﷺ) was specifying Mary and Āsiya, preferring these two above other women who have been vouchsafed prophecy. To show that some human beings are preferred above others, Ibn Ḥazm quotes the following text:

> Those messengers: We have preferred [*faḍḍalnā*] some above others;—of them there are those unto whom God spoke; and He exalted some of them in degrees [above others] . . . (2:253)

Having considered the matter from various perspectives, Ibn Ḥazm concludes:

> There are individuals whom God made more excellent than others, such as the prophets Muḥammad and

> Abraham, according to what has been transmitted to us; and the perfection of Mary and Āsiya over other women is confirmed by the Prophet's ḥadīth.[255]

Rāzī, however, draws a distinction between prophet and *walī*, stating that a prophet is governed by what is outwardly apparent, while the *walī* is governed by what is inwardly hidden.[256] But he differentiates between divinely-guided 'inspiration' and 'revelation'. To illuminate the difference, he quotes al-Ḥasan al-Baṣrī's statement that:

> Ḥanna vowed to consecrate her child as a result of an inspiration from God, just as Abraham beheld the sacrifice of his son in a dream and knew that it was a divine commandment, although it was not a revelation; just as the mother of Moses was inspired, and she cast him afloat, and it was not revelation.[257]

Rāzī thus accepts the position of those who reject Marian prophecy on the basis of 'And We sent not before thee [any messenger] save men'; he sees her as one of the saints (*awliyā'*), and describes the annunciation as a form of inspiration.[258] However, in his concluding remarks, Rāzī mentions that God accepted Mary's consecration to the Temple even though she was a female, and this had never been done before, and that God granted her Jesus without a father. Noting the extraordinary experiences of Mary, including the fact that God allowed her to hear the speech of the angel, Rāzī asserts that 'Mary, the *waliyya*, is preferred above *all* women'.[259]

This secondary controversy amongst some Sunni scholars is refined by some Sufis among them to a question over whether or not Mary should be classified as a prophetess or a saintly, holy woman (*waliyya*), primarily based on their understanding of the nature and purpose of miracles, and the application of this understanding to the differentiation between a prophet and a saint.

Qushayrī, combining the legalist and Sufi approach, details a difference between *nabī* and *walī*, focussing on categories of miracles as the determining factor. He begins by stating that the doctrine of the appearance of *karāmāt* (miracles worked through the *awliyā'*)[260] is theologically acceptable (*jā'iz*). Then, in an attempt to distinguish between different kinds of miracles, the *karāmāt* and the *muʿjizāt*, he quotes Imām Abū Isḥāq al-Isfarā'īnī,[261] saying:

> The *muʿjizāt* are proof-signs of prophethood, and the signs of prophecy are not found in anyone who is not a prophet. The *awliyā'* possess *karāmāt* which are similar to the answer to a prayer [*duʿā'*], while the *muʿjiza* is peculiar to prophets.[262]

He goes on to quote Imām Abū Bakr ibn Fūrak,[263] whose statement implies that the difference lies in the nature of the miracle itself. If the miracle calls the person to prophethood, then it is a *muʿjiza,* and if it directs the person towards sainthood, it is a *karāma*. Ibn Fūrak notes:

> Among the differences between the *muʿjizāt* and the *karāmāt* is [the fact] that prophets are commanded to display miracles, while the *awliyā'* [saints] must shield and hide them. And a prophet openly affirms his miracles, and thereby terminates discussion [about the matter], while a *walī* does not do either for fear that doing so may be deceptive. The *muʿjizāt* are uniquely for prophets, while the *karāmāt* are for the *awliyā'* because one of the conditions of [determining whether it is] a *muʿjiza* is dependent on the call of prophethood by way of the miracle. A *muʿjiza* is not established as such based on one condition only; it depends on many factors, and when one of the essential conditions is missing, it is not a *muʿjiza*. Clear, ascertained prophethood is one of these conditions.[264]

Qushayrī observes that the preconditions necessary for prophetic evidentiary miracles (*muʿjizāt*) are therefore found also in miracles given to saints (*karāmāt*), with the exception of the one condition of the presence of authentically ascertained prophethood. He adds that the *karāma* is an occurrence of something novel, which has not been previously attributed to someone else, and is unusual in its time. It appears to a selected servant of God, as a blessing, and it comes as a result of his desire and request (*duʿāʾ*) for it.[265] In other words, Qushayrī's view appears to be that the existence of a miracle is not in itself proof of prophethood; however, proof of prophethood is dependent on the existence of a miracle because prophets are sent to mankind, and miracles for them constitute proof of their mission. The *walī*, however, is not 'sent' to mankind, and thus, since miracles can be attributed to a *walī*, Mary would necessarily fit into the class of the saintly friends of God: she is a *waliyya*.

Adding a linguistic analysis, Qushayrī says that the word *walī* is of the *faʿīl* paradigm, which functions as an intensive form of the present participle (*fāʿil*), the form used for stressing and strengthening meaning, as, for example, *ʿalīm* and *qadīr*. Therefore it means: one who lives an uninterrupted life of obedience to God without a lapse into rebelliousness. He also adds the possibility that the intensive form of the present participle *faʿīl* has the meaning of *mafʿūl* (the passive participle), like *qatīl* (killed) in the sense of *maqtūl*, and *jarīḥ* (wounded) meaning *majrūḥ*. Thus the *walī* would be the one who is entrusted with the Truth by God, thanks to His protection from rebelliousness and disobedience so that his faith—his ability to be obedient—remains constant.[266] Qushayrī then mentions two aspects of the *walī*: firstly, that saints are not categorically protected from sin, which implies that in his categorization of Mary as *waliyya* he is discounting the sound ḥadīth which indicates that both Mary and her son have not been touched by Satan; and secondly, that a *walī* should experience fear when a miracle involving him occurs.[267] Further into his account, Qushayrī offers the following list of the *walī*'s characteristics:

> (1) Trust and faith in the truth of the divine realities; (2) compassionate companionship with all mankind, whatever their status or condition may be; (3) constancy of dealing with men with the best of manners and requesting the best for them from God without asking anything from them; (4) the explaining of important matters to help mankind to purge vengeance from them; (5) being the recipient of God's protection from any conscious resentment or envy

> of the wealth of others and the absence of greedy ambition of any kind; (6) guarding the tongue from evil with respect to others; (7) upholding testimony to man's [spiritual] equality; (8) not being an adversary to anyone in this world or the hereafter.[268]

Mary, who was the archetypal symbol of submission and obedience, who trusted totally in the Word of her Lord, who had no desire for the material world and who endured the fear of her people's slander but was protected by God, well represents for Qushayrī the category of saint (*waliyya*). Following his theoretical discussion of the miracles of saints, the first example he gives is that of Mary, of whom he says that she was neither a prophet nor a messenger, citing the description in 3:37 of her miraculous sustenance through the date palm and the spring as an example of the miracles of saints.[269] But while Qushayrī's classification of Mary as *waliyya* indicates his great reverence for her, it excludes consideration of the appearance of Gabriel (عليه السلام) and the fact of the communication of divine utterances to her via an angelic intermediary. The implication of his discussion of the differences between *muʿjizāt* and *karāmāt* is that he would consider these miracles to fall into the latter category as Mary was not a messenger sent with a mission to mankind. Furthermore, his repeated affirmation in his commentary, the *Laṭāʾif*,[270] that Mary was preferred over all the women of her time, clearly indicates that he does not consider her miracles to be prophetic *muʿjizāt* because if he did, he would have considered her preferred over the women of *all* times.

The eighteenth-century Indian sage Shāh Walī Allāh focusses on miracles as a determining factor, but also stresses the question of the directness or indirectness of the Message.[271] According to Baljon, Shāh Walī Allāh establishes three supra-ordinary categories of human being. At the summit is the prophet or the 'active intellect' (*al-ʿaql bi'l-fiʿl*).[272] The intermediary category is the *ḥakīm* (sage) or the 'materialised intellect' (*al-ʿaql al-hayūlī*). The lowest category above that of normal unregenerated humanity is the ascetic *walī*, austerely approaching the divine through purification of his soul and thus liberating the innermost, hidden centre of his heart, which is described as the Secret (*sirr*).[273] Shāh Walī Allāh says:

> The tongue of God appears to be adaptable to different dispositions of an individual. At one time, someone may receive a personal Message; at another time, a communication for general use. Thus the information which is obtained always fits a particular situation.[274]

A prophet, he says, receives instructions directly from God. A *ḥakīm* receives them indirectly, on a transcendental level. The *walī* also receives them indirectly, but through the innermost heart (*sirr*).[275] Shāh Walī Allāh includes Mary as having a quality of 'maleness', which he attributes to Ḥanna's desire for a male child. Thus, Mary was born with a 'virile' disposition—'She gained a strong body, a fine harmonious temperament, a sensitive religiousness and a fine purity.'[276] To confirm Mary's perfection, he quotes the ḥadīth 'Among men, there are many who have been perfect . . .'

He then focusses on the miracles associated with Mary. He mentions: (1) the provisions she received in her *miḥrāb*: the fruits of winter in summer and vice versa; (2) that Mary's birth, like that of the prophets John (عليه السلام) and Jesus (عليه السلام), was miraculous; (3) the signs that God gave to Mary after Jesus's birth—when the angel announced to her the perfections God would bestow on Jesus (3:45), the provision of the dates from the palm tree and water from the spring (19:24-26), and the fact that when Mary was falsely accused of fornication, God put words of exoneration into the mouth of the infant (19:28-32).[277] Thus, from Shāh Walī Allāh's detailed description of the miracles associated with Mary within the context of his discussion about symbols (*rumūz*) that 'indicate' the prophets, it appears that he considers her to be a prophetess.

We also encounter some commentators who refrain from entering the controversy outlined in this chapter. In Ibn ʿArabī's explication of 19:3; 24-25, he summarises the blessings she received. For him, two of the most important are the 'witnessing' of her Lord for her by means of the falling of the dates from the desiccated palm tree, and the speaking of the babe in his cradle. He describes her as being 'for God [*li'Llāh*], by God [*bi'Llāh*], and on the authority of God [*ʿani'Llāh*].'[278] In other words, she was God's total slave. She served her Lord, loved her Lord, and knew her Lord; and her Lord loved her. 'For this reason, Zachariah, the prophet of God, was envious of her, and wanted [blessings] from God similar to those which she had received, so he "cried out to his Lord secretly".'[279] Ibn ʿArabī centres his gloss to 19:21 on Mary's unique spirituality. Having stated that woman is not normally charged with the task of making the connection between the knowledge of the Oneness of the Essence *(aḥadiyyat al-dhātiyya)* and the perception and knowledge of God's Godly Being, which is the Unity of the Many, he goes on to state that this was indeed Mary's state. 'Thus,' he says, 'she is among those who attained the state of perfection [*kamāl*].'[280]

Rūzbihān Baqlī's interpretation of 19:16 provides a penetrating description of the spiritual achievement of Mary, 'the perfect,' and an understanding of why she is such an important figure in Islam:

> The true indication here [of 19:16] is that the essence of Mary is the essence of the holy *fiṭra* [primordial human nature]. And her essence was trained by 'the Real',[281] by the light of intimacy. And in all of her respirations [in every breath], she was *majdhūba*[282] by the attribute of the closeness and intimacy to the Source of Divine Illumination. She became constantly in a state of spiritual vigilance [*murāqaba*][283] for the manifestation of the illumination of the World of Sovereignty[284] [*jabarūt*],[285] from the point of the rising place of spiritual orientation [*mashriq*][286] in the realm of the Kingdom [*malakūt*].[287] And she withdrew from the world via spiritual resolve [*himma*][288] of the highest category, characterised by the light of the Unseen. And she approached the rising-places [*mashāriq*] of the Illumination of the Essence [*dhāt*],[289] and she inhaled the Attributes—fragrances from the Eternal World without beginning [*ʿālam al-azal*][290]. And the gift reached her—the communion with the Pre-Eternal [*azaliyya*]. And the Illumination of the 'witnessing of the

> Eternal' [*mushāhadat al-qidamiyya*][291] shone upon her. And when she experienced the vision of the Illumination of the Manifestation of Eternity, Its Lights flashed, and Its Secrets reached her spirit [*rūḥ*], and her spirit became impregnated with the Divine Secret, and she became the bearer of the glorious word[292] and the light of the spirit of the Most High. And when her state became magnified with the reflection of the beauty of the Illumination of Eternity upon her, she concealed herself out of fear [of people] and withdrew [from them] with the 'bridegroom' of[293] the Reality [*al-ḥaqīqa*][294,295]

In his commentary, Rūzbihān reiterates the point that the development of Mary's great spirituality and her subsequent spiritual achievement *preceded* the miraculous conception of Jesus. From his description, it appears that the latter could not have happened without the prior purification of the heart and that this in fact was Mary's natural disposition—that she was born to be the pure essence of the *fiṭra*[296] and to be imbued with secrets of the Eternal. This is a description of a Mary who is not revered solely as the mother of a prophet and a messenger, but who is chosen to be a spiritual luminary in her own right, through Divine guidance, spiritual exercise, the awareness of blessings which drew her closer and closer into the reflection of the Light of her Lord, and the ability to act on such perception. Her life, then, up to the point just prior to the miraculous conception is a model of perfect piety, faith and trust in her Lord; and her 'witnessing' of the Unseen World of the Angels, leading to the disclosure of its secrets certainly places her in the highest category of spiritual luminaries.

Looking back at the controversy, the contemporary theologian ʿAbd al-Salām Badawī also refrains from passing judgement, merely opining that the evident sense of the Qur'ān and ḥadīth leads to the conclusion that

> Mary is the most preferred of all women of the world, from Eve to the last woman who shall exist, and that: (1) the angel brought her revelation from God—a commandment from

God, a Message and good news as was brought to all the prophets; (2) God especially chose Mary for an experience for which no other woman was chosen—the Holy Spirit spoke to her, appeared to her, and blew into the pit of her garment; (3) she believed acceptingly in the words of her Lord, without asking for a sign, as Zachariah had done, when she was given the good news from God about the Messiah, and as a result God bestowed upon her the title of *ṣiddīqa* [the sincere of faith]. Thus, God was a witness for her being the *ṣiddīqa*, as He was for her being the *qanūt* [the obedient].[297]

The arguments outlined in this chapter indicate that in the key territories of the Islamic world, through the medieval period and into more contemporary times, considerable and unresolved controversy over Mary's precise spiritual status has persisted amongst Muslim thinkers. The strongest and most cohesive arguments have been put forward by those who accept Mary's prophethood, as they are clearly based on a logical understanding of the Qur'ānic passages and the sound ḥadīths, while those who reject her prophethood have used arguments which appear to be unconvincing, or even specious.

Designating Mary as the saintly friend of Allah, as *waliyya*, is a natural and justifiable extension of her scriptural title of *ṣiddīqa*; however, as a formal categorisation, this excludes the manifestly prophetic quality of her miracles. Essentially, for those who consider there to be no distinction between a prophet and a messenger of God, Mary cannot be a prophetess. For those who see the distinction lying in the fact that a prophet is one who receives revelation via an angelic intermediary, while a messenger is one who has been singled out to warn, guide or otherwise set before a particular community a divine message which has been revealed to him,[298] then Mary is a prophetess, but not a messenger, as she certainly received revelation directly from the Archangel, but was not given a specific message, nor a Book, such as the Qur'ān, the Injīl, or the Torah, to convey to mankind. Instead, Mary was miraculously *given* a messenger, Jesus. Seyyed Hossein Nasr's description of Mary's role in Christianity as the vehicle of the Divine Message[299] is comparable to the traditional Islamic view of Jesus as the bearer of a Divine Message and Mary as the 'immaculate' vehicle.[300] Thus, Mary was an intricate part of the process by which the message was conveyed, and forms, together with her son, one symbolic 'sign' to humanity.

We might add the following. Mary figures in the Qur'ānic chapter of the Prophets (*al-Anbiyā'*) along with others who are universally accepted in Islam as prophets; and she is included with the prophets in the chapter which bears her own name, and which closes with the words, 'Those were they to whom God showed favour among the prophets . . .' (19:58) The fact remains, however, that the individuals who are mentioned in the Chapter of Mary fall into one of the following categories. Firstly, that of the righteous, the sincere of faith (*ṣiddīq*) who is a prophet (*nabī*). Secondly, the prophet and messenger (*rasūl*). Thirdly, the prophet who is not a messenger, except Mary, who is called '*ṣiddīqa*' only. It would appear then that all the others are clearly established as prophets, while whether or not Mary is a prophetess is not actually demonstrated.[301] Consequently the conclusion which can be drawn is that God chose Mary to be a symbol of obedience and submission, the most righteous, the most saintly, the purest and the most perfect of the women of all times. Furthermore, as she had the attributes and the experiences of prophets, and there is no satisfactory argument against her having achieved their status, she should be logically classified as a prophetess, although this should not be regarded as proven beyond dispute.

CHAPTER SIX

Conclusion

M ARY (﷽) in traditional Sunni Islam is an important figure in herself. Her position is not just that of the most exalted category of women, but she is ranked in the highest category of all human beings. In fact, from the perspective of those scholars who consider Mary to be a prophetess, she is considered equal to this aspect of her son Jesus (عليه السلام). And to those who focus on Mary's outstanding spiritual achievements, she is seen to have been blessed with stages of spiritual development that approach those of the Prophet Muḥammad (ﷺ). In no case is Mary seen solely as the mother of Jesus. Rather, a reverse attitude seems to prevail. It is the consistent image of Jesus as the *son* of Mary (which is a constant denial of an image of Jesus as the 'Son of God') that remains in mind because this constitutes the essential doctrinal point which affirms the Qur'ānic proclamation of the pure Oneness of God and the subordination of all His creatures: angels, jinns, mankind—including prophets. Mary and her son form a reminder of God's unique fiat and power. Together they are one of the many signs which the Qur'ān sets forth, in order to disentangle man from mere earthly concerns (*dunyā*), and to preserve him from the belief that only what he sees is what is, veiled from the limitless possibilities.

According to the classical Sunni scholars, Mary is, thus, by virtue of God's will, a spiritual luminary who in her primary role as woman slave of God became an ideal of sincerity, faith, devoutness, submission and purity, and who by virtue of these characteristics was opened to God's eternal word and then granted the secondary role of mother. Mary is, therefore, a sign for all Muslim believers, male or female.

This becomes even more apparent when the texts of 3:17 and 33:35 are considered. For in these passages, characteristics of which the Virgin is an ideal example are specified as paradigms for all believers. The Qur'ān lists the following candidates for Paradise:

> The patient and the steadfast, the truthful and the obedient, those who spend [in the cause of God], and those who pray for forgiveness in the early morning hours. (3:17)

The Qur'ān further provides the following a general address to all those who surrender to the divine will:

> Assuredly, for Muslim men and Muslim women
> [those who surrender to God]
> For believing men and believing women,
> For devout men and devout women,
> For truthful men and truthful women,
> For men who persevere [in righteousness]
> and women who persevere,
> For humble men and humble women,
> For men who give alms and women who give alms,
> For men who fast and women who fast,
> For men who guard their chastity
> and women who guard their chastity,
> For men who remember God much,
> and for women who remember:
> God has prepared for them forgiveness
> and a great reward. (33:35)

Thus in Marian spirituality Muslims contemplate the living image of a human embodiment of the traits which they strive to achieve. Mary, the 'perfect,' the 'complete' is relevant to the lives of believers, who know that despite their faults, God is Merciful and Capable of all things. Thus, they pray to be endowed with the characteristics of Mary and to be recipients of similar blessings. They hope to be blessed in their circumstances and needs, as Mary was blessed, just as Zachariah (عﻠﻴﻪ) was inspired to pray for a son in his old age when he saw Mary's miraculous provisions. He did not pray for the same miracle that had been bestowed upon Mary, but for a miracle for himself from the Provider of all miracles. Consequently, Mary's story has been defended in times of opposition, and has been shared in times of peace. It has formed the basis of a rich heritage of prayers, songs and poetry.

A popular example is the *dīwān*[302] found by E. Littmann which comprises a fairly accurate reproduction of the accepted scholarly version of the life of Mary. Littman's assumption is that it was recited in colloquial Egyptian Arabic to the accompaniment of the tambourine.[303]

In the seventh century, it was the early Qur'ānic account of Mary that spared the lives of an important group of Muslims. In the year after the first emigration to Christian Abyssinia in 615, a relatively small band of Muslims who had escaped from their oppressors in Mecca were sent back to Abyssinia by the Prophet, and it was the recitation of the Qur'ānic passages about Mary[304] that forged a bond between the two communities and afforded the Muslims safe refuge for approximately fourteen years.[305]

To take a further instance: this time from sixteenth-century Spain: in the literature of the Moriscos,[306] we encounter very abundant mention of Mary.[307] Puey Monzón, a Morisco with the soubriquet of Alhichante (sc. *al-ḥajjī*),[308] composed an account of his pilgrimage to Makka in strophic verse.[309] Performing the *ḥajj* (the greater Pilgrimage) afforded Puey Monzón the opportunity to visit some of the traditional sites of Mary and Jesus in the vicinity of Cairo,[310] and he includes a description in verse of one such site and the *qiṣaṣ* popularly associated with it in Egypt:[311]

no. xxx: We went out travelling
From Cairo one day,
By the river at the foot of
The road of Maṭariyya
To see an orchard where there stood
An ancient fig tree[312]
That for more than seventeen hundred years
In this orchard remained.

no. xxxi: That which opened for Mary,
With certitude, in order to save her,
When the false Jews
Went out to kill her:
She and her son,
It placed them in the Heart,
That which seven times a year
Bears fruit as a blessing.[313]

Pano y Ruata associates the poet's account with the famous sycamore tree in whose shade, according to the *qiṣaṣ*, the holy family rested during the flight from Herod.[314] In Puey Monzón's verse, we observe a focus on Mary herself, for it is Mary for whom the tree opened; Mary who was to be saved from her pursuers; and Mary and her son who were 'placed in the Heart'.

Mary is also a focus in the traditional *duʿā'* (voluntary supplication) of the Moriscos. As part of the ritual Friday congregational service, after the second *aljotba*,[315] in the *duʿā'* led by the imām, God is asked to accept their gratitude for His blessings upon them. Amongst the detailed blessings mentioned is: '*por la datilera de Mary*'[316] (for the date palm of Mary), the hope being that God will be as clement, merciful, and generous to them as He was to the Virgin. In private, when offering longer individual *duʿā'*s, the Moriscos included mention of God's blessings to the angels and to the prophets, from Adam to Muḥammad, a large portion of which is devoted to Mary:[317]

A *du'ā'* of Much Virtue and Just Recompense

... Zachariah (ﷺ); and for
the supplications in the Holy Sanctuary when
he tutored Mary; ...
and for the Benevolence that You
placed upon Mary (ﷺ), that You
appointed her and chose her and purified her above all
women, and for the excellent supplications
that she made to You in her *miḥrāb* and in the Holy
Sanctuary, and under the date palm where
she was in labour, and she found herself in great anxiety and
fear of the Jews who wanted
to kill her; and for the Benevolence that You
placed upon 'Īsā (ﷺ), by [Your] saying
'Be' [and] then 'It was'; and You blew into Mary of Your
Spirit, and she was impregnated
without the touch [being corrupted by] of a male, with great
purity ...

This extensive section of a Spanish-language prayer devoted to Mary indicates her great importance to the Moriscos as a model of devoutness, purity, patience, submissiveness, and above all as a sign of God's Power in and over all things.

El Mancebo de Arévolo, another Morisco scholar, includes in his Qur'ānic commentary[318] a section entitled 'The Superior Virtues of Mary', which appears to have been inspired by the works of Ibn 'Arabī and al-Ghazālī. In his commentary, El Mancebo produces levels of meanings, creates images and binds the Spanish word to the Arabic-Islamic concept in an attempt to describe the great spirituality attributed to Mary in Islam.[319]

The Superior Virtues of Mary

Mary, the daughter of 'Imrān, did not have the fire of physical passion,[320] and thus the Arabs say that stimulation of the flesh did not touch her[321] and that she was *but* [*a*]*tiva* [consecrated][322] spiritually, thus speaking clearly and frankly, that is to say, [the] secluded one who withdrew from the temporal world [out of] spiritual resolve.[323] And her corporeal desire remained barren, that is to say, frozen, such that no case [has] possessed as [spiritually] powerful nor comparably illustrious an act [deed]. And for this Spiritual Path,[324] Mary was adopted,[325] spiritual, enchased[326] in a simple enclosure, and the angels did not take her as [their] charge in the manner of a nun[327] of a Patriarchate, rather they visited her as a 'dubical'[328] figure. And they gave her celestial adornments,[329] that is to say, divine grace [inspiration] of the Essence[330] even as the slaves[331] [of God], the prophets, received. And God guarded her from harm[332] and placed a barrier [333] over her that is an invisible light of protection,[334] not of the eyes but of the hearts,[335] and [her heart] filled with spiritual somnolence [*lannas*][336] that sets the hearts [souls] to rest.

From the perspective of the classical Muslim scholars, Mary, in the Qur'ān and Sunna, is a symbol that brings together all revelation. As a descendant of the great Israelite prophets, the bearer of the word, the mother of Jesus, and as traditional Sunni Islam's chosen woman of all the worlds, Mary is symbolic of the Qur'anic message that revelation has not been confined to one particular people.[337] This symbolism is embodied in the placement of part of 3:37 above many a prayer-niche (*miḥrāb*),[338] including that of the Juyūshī Mosque,[339] one of the oldest Fāṭimid mosques in Cairo:

> . . . He [Zachariah] said: O Mary! Whence [comes] this to you? She said: It is from God. God provides sustenance to whom He pleases without measure. (3:37)

This *āya* summarises Mary's contentment in prayer in her sanctuary (*miḥrāb*) and the subsequent blessings she received from her Lord. Thus, the second *qibla*[340] is a reminder of the first *qibla*,[341] the site of Mary's *miḥrāb*, which was a test of sincerity of faith and submission to the Will of God—*Islām*.

APPENDIX

Pictures in the Kaʿba

IN PRE-ISLAMIC times, Makka also contained the idols of foreigners, and thus was a centre of pilgrimage for the whole peninsula. This provided a regular source of income for the inhabitants of Makka. Evidence of pre-Islamic, Christian pilgrimage to Makka was found inside the Kaʿba when the Muslims took the city in 630 AD.[1] Parrinder recounts al-Azraqī's story that the Prophet (ﷺ) demanded the cleansing of the Kaʿba of all pictures, except that of Mary (عليها السلام), and the babe, Jesus (عليه السلام) and that it remained there until the Kaʿba was destroyed by burning in 683.[2] The following is a discussion of the al-Azraqī story and the editor Mulḥas' refutation of the veracity of this account.

Al-Azraqī, who is not renowned as a ḥadīth scholar, includes the following account without mentioning his sources:[3]

1. In the Kaʿba, there were pictures of the prophets, and pictures of trees (*shajar*) and pictures of angels, and there was a picture of Ibrāhīm al-Khalīl[4] . . . and a picture of ʿĪsā ibn Maryam and his mother, and a picture of the angels. So when it was the Day of the Opening of Makka, the Messenger of God (ﷺ) entered, and he sent al-Faḍl ibn al-ʿAbbās ibn ʿAbd al-Muṭṭalib to get the water of Zamzam, then he ordered a piece of cloth, and he ordered the erasing of these pictures, and they were erased.

2. *The account continues:*

 He said: And he put his hand over the picture of ʿĪsā ibn Maryam and his mother, and he said: Wipe away all of the pictures except what is under my hand and he raised his hand up from ʿĪsā ibn Maryam and his mother.

3. *And further:*

 And looked at the picture of Abraham and said: May God strike them dead! They drew him casting lots with arrows. What is the connection between Abraham and the arrows?[5]

Mulḥas states that Section (2) of this account: 'Is an added insertion, which is not found in any of the ḥadīth transmitted by the Companions of the Sunan, about the pictures and images in the Kaʿba, and its text is rejected (*matrūk*) and erroneous (*bāṭil*).'[6] He begins his proof with a ḥadīth from the collection of al-Bukhārī:

> On the authority of Ibn ʿAbbās, he said: When the Messenger of God (ﷺ) entered Makka, he refused to go inside the House (Kaʿba) while there were still gods in it. And he stated his orders, and they were removed, and a picture of Abraham and Ishmael with the arrows (lots) in their hands was removed. And the Prophet (ﷺ) said: May God strike them dead. Surely, they knew that they (Abraham and Ishmael) *never* cast lots! Then, he entered the House, and said Allāhu Akbar in every part of the House and departed without praying in it. (al-Bukhārī)[7]

Mulḥas quotes this ḥadīth to show that this sound collection does not include Section (2) of the al-Azraqī account. In Ibn Ḥajar's commentary on this ḥadīth he mentions two addtional accounts, similar to al-Azraqī's by writers of *qiṣaṣ* and other non-ḥadīth scholars, which he clearly dismisses, preferring the ḥadīths with sound chains of authority which state that all the pictures inside the Kaʿba were erased on the Day of the Opening of Makka.[8]

In addition to the ḥadīth mentioned by Mulḥas, there is the following sound ḥadīth from the collection of Abū Dāwūd:

> Ibrāhīm (i.e. Ibn ʿAqīl) said: on the authority of Wahb ibn Munabbih, on the authority of Jābir, he said: that the Prophet (ﷺ) ordered ʿUmar ibn al-Khaṭṭāb, at the time of the Opening (of Makka), while he was in the valley, to go to the Kaʿba and erase every picture in it. And the Prophet (ﷺ) did not enter it until it was cleansed of every picture in it. (Abū Dāwūd)[9]

Thus, a further indication of the correctness of Mulḥas' conclusion that leaving the picture of Mary and Jesus was a later insertion is the fact that although al-Azraqī states that he usually relies on Wahb, this sound ḥadīth which was transmittted by Wahb states that *all* pictures were erased.

Al-Wāqidī, in his Maghāzī, mentions various accounts of the incident, one of which states that ʿUmar was ordered to erase all the pictures, and did so with the exception of Abraham's, and upon seeing it, the Prophet (ﷺ) ordered: Well, destroy it. However, it is clear that al-Wāqidī does not accept this account, as it begins with the vague: They said.[10] The following account is obviously preferred by al-Wāqidī, as it is the final one mentioned, and he provides its full chain of authorities (*isnād*):

> Al-Wāqidī said: Ibn Abī Dhi'b reported to him (with his *isnād*) on the authority of Usāma ibn Zayd, he said: I entered the Kaʿba with the Messenger of God (ﷺ), and he saw pictures in it, so he ordered me to bring him a bucket of water, then he wet a piece of cloth with it and destroyed the pictures. And he said: May God strike dead a people who make pictures of that which they have not created![11]

Mulḥas continues his argument by making the point that such behaviour, i.e. leaving the picture of Mary and Jesus inside the Kaʿba would be *munkar* (legally reproachable, detestable, forbidden behaviour), and that obviously, the Prophet ﷺ would never decide to do something categorised as *munkar*.[12] Mulḥas adds that: The Prophet ﷺ would not wish to be separated from the angels, and they do not enter a house with pictures.[13] Indeed there are numerous ḥadīths about this point,and others which clarify the spiritual loss accruing to the maker of pictures and other images:

> On the authority of ʿAlī, he said, the Prophet ﷺ said: The angels do not enter a house with a dog or picture. (Aḥmad ibn Ḥanbal; al-Bukhārī; Muslim, Abū Dāwūd; al-Nasā'ī)[14]

Al-Nawawī specifies the kind of picture that is being referred to: It is said that this reference is to the punishment for one who makes a picture, intending that it be worshipped, and that goes for statues, etc.[15] He adds that according to the scholars in the making of such pictures, there is an attempted correspondence to the characteristic of Allah, the Most High, as Creator, and this is a major sin of impudence and disobedience.[16]

The following is an example of a ḥadīth expressing the spiritual loss to the painter of such pictures:

> On the authority of ʿĀ'isha: Umm Ḥabība and Umm Salama mentioned a church they had seen in Abyssinia in which there were pictures (images), and they mentioned this to the Prophet. So, he (ﷺ) said that if [i.e. when] there is a righteous man amongst those people, and he dies, they build a house of worship over his grave and paint such pictures in it. They will be the worst of (the) creatures to God on the Day of Resurrection. (al-Bukhārī)[17]

An excerpt from one final ḥadīth exemplifies that even if the picture is of one as saintly as Maryam—or rather because that is the case, and thus might be worshipped or expected to provide intercession, it is rejected:

> On the authority of Muslim ibn Ṣubayḥ, he said: I was with Masrūq in a house which had portraits of Maryam, and Masrūq said: these are portraits of Kisrā (i.e. the Persian king), and I said: these are portraits of Maryam. So, Masrūq said: But, I heard ʿAbdullāh ibn Masʿūd say, the Messenger of Allah ﷺ said: the people who will receive the greatest punishment on the Day of Resurrection are the painters of pictures . . .(Muslim)[18]

It seems apparent, both from the perspective of reliability of sources, and in light of the great quantity of reliable evidence available, that al-Azraqī's account is fallacious with respect to Section (2), which indeed must have been a later insertion, perhaps from an Isrā'īlī source. This conclusion is underscored by the fact that notwithstanding the great love and respect that traditional Sunni Islam has for both Mary and Jesus, the abhorrence and forbidding of images intended for worship would render it impossible for the Prophet of this spiritual community (*umma*) to jeopardise his status on the Day of Resurrection for the sake of these sentiments. Furthermore, such an act would have influenced millions of his followers, from the time of the Prophet (ﷺ) to today, to disobey the ordinance against what Mulḥas describes as *shirk* (polytheism),[19] while, in fact, the opposite is true, as Muslim *qādīs*[20] still give dispensations as to which pictures are *mubāḥ* (permissible, without harm or good) and which are *ḥarām* (forbidden). Thus the possibility that pictures of the saintly Mary (ﷺ), or any of the prophets (ﷺ), would be revered to the degree of worship or used as a vehicle for intercession is sufficient cause in Islam to forbid their display.[21]

Notes

1 Qur'ān: 50:45; 17:9; 16:64 and others.

2 Arabic names: Ibrāhīm, Ismāʿīl, Isḥāq, Yaʿqūb, Mūsā, ʿĪsā.

3 *Ahl al-Kitāb*: the people to whom God gave Scripture, i.e., Jews and Christians.

4 *Ṣaḥīḥ al-Bukhārī* in Ibn Ḥajar, *Fatḥ*, VIII, 170, Kitāb al-Tafsīr, Bāb XI (no. 4485).

5 Qurṭubī, *Jāmiʿ*, IV,62.

6 The elements in parentheses are sometimes found after Dāwūd. For detailed differences see Ibn Kathīr, *Tafsīr* i,358; Ṭabarī, *Jāmiʿ*, III, 235; Thaʿlabī, *Qiṣaṣ*, 207. For the variation ʿImrān ibn Māthān,see Ibn Saʿd, *Ṭabaqāt,* I, 55; Zamakhsharī, *Kashshāf,* I, 141; and the reference to Suhaylī in Qurṭubī, *Jamiʿ*, IV, 62.

7 Ibid., Ibn Kathīr, *Tafsīr,* 359; Thaʿlabī; Zamakhsharī. Ṭabarī, *Jāmiʿ*, adds: Ḥanna bint Fāqūdh ibn Qatīl. Muqātil, *Tafsīr,* 166, adds that she is from the line of David.

8 See Ibn Kathīr, *Tafsīr,* I, 359; Qurṭubī, *Jāmiʿ*, IV, 66; Suyūṭī and Maḥallī, *Tafsīr al-Jalalayn* (margin of Bayḍāwī), I, 113; Ibn Hishām, *Sīra,* II, 163; Muqātil, *Tafsīr,* 166.

9 Bayt al-Maqdis (the Holy Enclosure) may refer to the greater area of Jerusalem, or to the *Ḥaram al-Sharīf* (the walled area, including the Dome of the Rock and the Aqsa Mosque), or to the Temple area of the time of Mary, which is the meaning here. See S. A. Schleifer, 'Islamic Jerusalem,' 163-64 for discussion of the Islamic perspective of the 'spiritual geography' of Jerusalem. Here Bayt al-Maqdis refers to the ancient Temple site.

10 Ṭabarī, *Jāmiʿ*, III, 235-36 (Attributed to Ibn Isḥāq, and to al-Qāsim, on the authority of ʿIkrīma and Abū Bakr); Ṭabarī, *Tārīkh,* I, 141-42.

11 Zamakhsharī, *Kashshāf*, I, 141–42.

12 Zamakhsharī, *Kashshāf*, I, 142. Rāzī, *Mafātīḥ*, II, 457; Mūqātil, *Tafsīr*, 167; Ibn al-Athīr, *Kāmil*, I, 298; Thaʿlabī, *Qiṣaṣ*, 207–8; Ibn Kathīr says that directly following Ḥanna's prayer for a child, she mensruated, after which she became pregnant from the first incidence of sexual contact with her husband: *Qiṣaṣ*, II, 369.

13 Ibn Kathīr, *Tafsīr*, I, 359–60; Ṭabarī, *Jāmiʿ*, III, 235; Zamakhsharī, *Kashshāf*, I, 142; Ibn al-Athīr, *Tārīkh*, I, 298; Thaʿlabī, *Qiṣaṣ*, 208; Suyūṭī, *Itḥāf*, II, 14. According to the editor of the *Itḥāf*, Dr. Aḥmad Ramaḍān Aḥmad, scholars differ about the name of the author. He accepts the name: (Abū ʿAbdullāh) Muḥammad ibn (Shihāb al-Dīn) Aḥmad ibn ʿAlī ibn ʿAbd al-Khāliq al-Manhajī Shams ad-Dīn (813–80 AH), based on a Damascus manuscript and one owned by Ilyās Sarkīs, plus other reference books and the fact that the author himself mentions entering Jerusalem in 874 AH; others say it is: Kamāl ad-Dīn Muḥammad Maqdisī, usually known as Ibn Sharīf al-Shāfiʿī al-Miṣrī (d. 906 AH) or Jalāl al-Dīn ʿAbd al-Raḥmān ibn Abū Bakr al-Suyūṭī (849–911 AH) based on other extant manuscripts; see I, 15.

14 The above-mentioned details about the customary practice of consecrating the male child at that time are found in all discussions about Mary. Reasons for the choice of the male child have been suggested by some scholars, among whom is Maqdisī, who states menstruation, i.e., a regular period of ritual impurity, as being the primary reason for not choosing females: Maqdisī, *Bad'*, III, 118. Badawī, *Batūl*, 10.

15 Qurṭubī, *Jāmiʿ*, IV, 66.

16 *Jalalayn* (Bayḍāwī—margin), I, 113; Badawī, *Batūl*, 10; Zamakhsharī, *Kashshāf*, I, 142; Nasafī, *Tafsīr* I, 151; Ibn Ḥajar, *Fatḥ*, VI, 469, 'Maryam in Syriac means the one who serves.' *Encycl. Judaica*, XII, 82: 'Miriam (Heb.: perhaps "wish"; or Aramaic Maram, a compound of Egyptian "mer", meaning "love")'. *Shorter Encycl. of Islam*: 'Maryam: Arabic form of name identical with the Syriac and Greek, which are used in the Syriac and in the Greek Bible, in the New as well as in the Old Testament. In the latter it corresponds to the Hebrew', 327. Also see *Encycl. of Islam* (new ed.): 'The name Maryam, like others with the same suffix, such as ʿAmram, Bilʿam, points to the region between Palestine and northwestern Arabia as its home,' 628. Also: *New Columbia Encycl.*, 134: '*Aramaic*: By the beginning of the 17th century B.C., Aramaic had spread throughout the Fertile Crescent as a *lingua franca*. After the Jews

were defeated by the Babylonians in 586 B.C., they began to speak Aramaic instead of Hebrew, although they retained Hebrew as the sacred language of their religion. Aramaic was also the language of Jesus. In its long history, Aramaic broke up into dialects, one of which was Syriac. Parts of the books of Ezra and Daniel in the Old Testament were written in an Aramaic dialect, as were major portions of the Palestinian and Babylonian Talmuds.' Smith and Haddad, 'The Virgin', 164 suggest that the name is understood to be 'a confirmation of her mother's dedication of her.'

17 Qurṭubī, *Jāmiʿ*, IV, 71; Zamakhsharī, *Kashshāf*, I, 143; Bayḍāwī, *Tafsīr*, I, 113; Thaʿlabī, *Qiṣaṣ*, 208.

18 Zamakhsharī, *Kashshāf*, I, 143; Ibn al-Athīr, *Tārīkh*, I, 298; Thaʿlabī, *Qiṣaṣ*, 208.

19 Although most of the scholars say that Zachariah's wife, the mother of the prophet Yaḥyā (John) (عليه السلام), could have been either the sister of Ḥanna, i.e., Mary's aunt, or the sister of Mary herself, they always refer to her as Mary's aunt when recording this account. This is because the account goes back to Ibn Isḥāq who, along with Ibn Jarīr and others, is of the opinion that Zachariah was married to Mary's aunt. However, scholars do not all, personally, accept this view, or they remain undecided, because of the statement of the Prophet that 'Yaḥyā and ʿĪsā are maternal cousins,' which is found in the sound ḥadīth (See Ibn Kathīr, *Tafsīr*, I, 360; Suyūṭī, *Itḥāf*, II, 14; Ibn Qutayba, *Maʿārif*, 52. Also, perhaps since she is estimated to have been around 85 years old when Mary was born, others have preferred the opinion that she was Mary's aunt, or left the matter undecided; see Badawī, *Batūl*, 17. Her name is said to be similar to ʿAshyā'.

20 Ibn Kathīr, *Tafsīr*, I, 363; Thaʿlabī, *Qiṣaṣ*, 208. In the discussions about this matter, some simply say, 'a nearby river,' without further specification.

21 Usually understood to be 'arrows' although some say 'reeds,' i.e., the pens with which the scribe-rabbis wrote the Torah: See Qurṭubī, *Jāmiʿ*, IV, 86; Ibn Kathīr, *Tafsīr*, I, 363; Ṭabarī, *Jāmiʿ*, III, 241; 267; Thaʿlabī, *Qiṣaṣ*, 208. Both reeds and arrows appear to have been used at that time: see *New Schaff-Herzog Encycl.*, VII, 45: 'The lot takes the first place in ancient Israel as a means of seeking counsel of the Deity. In early times there existed various methods of casting lots, as by means of wooden staves or arrows: Hosea 4:12; Ezek. 21:21. Also, Matt. 27:35. It was usually the privilege of the priest to cast the lot.'

22 According to Ṭabarī, a *miḥrāb* is a place to sit and pray, and it is the best of such places, the most honoured and the most blessed, and thus is found in mosques; see Ṭabarī, *Jāmiʿ*, III, 246. In contemporary usage, *miḥrāb* is generally restricted to meaning: a recess in the wall of a mosque, etc., a prayer niche. Here the place referred to is a secluded room in the Temple (Bayt al-Maqdis), and according to Badawī it is so called because it is the place of *muḥāraba*, i.e., of combatting Satan.

23 Ibid., Badawī; Qurṭubī, *Jāmiʿ*, IV, 71.

24 Ṭabarī; *Jāmiʿ*, 244. The implication is that this food was brought to Mary by Gabriel (ﷺ) directly from heaven: see Muqātil, *Tafsīr*, 168.

25 Most scholars are of the opinion that Mary received these miraculous provisions from the time she was placed in her *miḥrāb*, i.e., from infancy. Rāzī, however, questions the nature of Zachariah's function as guardian, if every time he came, he found her already provided with sustenance. Therefore, he suggests that perhaps the miraculous provisions came later on, and in the early years, Zachariah himself provided Mary with food and drink. But, he ends his discussion by observing that some say the '*wāw*' ('and') connects the provision by God to the guardianship of Zachariah: 'and [her Lord] vouchsafed to her a goodly growth and made Zachariah her guardian'. (3:37), so perhaps they happened at the same time: see Rāzī, *Tafsīr*, II, 460. Also, Badawī, *Batūl*, 25. Also, re 'speaking as a babe', see Bayḍawī, I, 114; Zamakhsharī, *Kashshāf*, I, 143; Khāzin, *Tafsīr*, I, 225.

26 Ibn Kathīr, *Tafsīr*, I, 360; Badawī, *Batūl*, 16; Zamakhsharī, *Kashshāf*, I, 143; Thaʿlabī, *Qiṣaṣ*, 209.

27 According to Badawī, Zachariah was 120 years old and his wife was 98 when John the prophet (ﷺ) was conceived; see *Batūl*, 17.

28 Most scholars agree: Qurṭubī, *Jāmiʿ*, IV, 71; Muqātil, *Tafsīr*, 168; Zamakhsharī, *Kashshāf*, II, 4. Some have said she was purified of menstruation; Zajjāj: (Qurṭubī, *Jāmiʿ*, IV, 82; Rāzī, *Tafsīr*, II, 467.)

29 Ibn Kathīr, *Tafsīr*, III, 114 and *Qiṣaṣ*, II ,385.

30 Joseph is considered by some to have been the maternal cousin of Mary: Maqdisī, *Bad'* (Ar.), III, 119; Ibn Kathīr, *Qiṣaṣ*, II, 388, and by others to have been her paternal cousin: see Zamakhsharī, *Kashshāf*, II, 5; Badawī, *Batūl*, 42; Thaʿlabī, *Qiṣaṣ*, 298.

31 Ibn Hishām, *Sīra*, II, 163; Thaʿlabī, *Qiṣaṣ*, 208-209.

32 Ibn Hishām, *Sīra*, II, 163.

33 Thaʿlabī, *Qiṣaṣ*, 208–9.

34 Ibn Qutayba, *Maʿārif*, 53; Badawī, *Batūl*, 42 (relies on the Gospel of Barnabas).

35 Ibn Qayyim al-Jawziyya, *Hidāya*, 305–6. *Jewish Encycl.*, 2943–44 states that in ancient times endogamy prevailed as a custom although later there were political alliances through marriage with other tribes: Gen.24:2–4 and 29:19; Judges 14:3. L.M. Epstein, *Marriage Laws*, 146–47, mentions five reasons for the prohibition of intermarriage, which he describes as a custom or rule, although 'The law raises objection to marriage between man and woman of different Hebrew tribes only where it becomes the cause of conveying property from one tribe to another'. But, he notes that 'The rule of endogamy was much sharper in the case of priests.' (308–9) Graves, *Nazarene*, 50, emphasises this point: 'But it is unlikely that a daughter of a priestly house in Jerusalem would have married a Galilean carpenter, even a scion of the House of David. Priests' daughters were notoriously proud of their descent from Aaron, and though the Mosaic ban on inter-tribal marriages (Numbers 36:8–9), had now been repealed by the Pharisees (Ta'anith 30b), it seems to have still kept a certain superstitious force.' He adds: 'Scripture advised these daughters to marry only such as were worthy of them. (Baba Bathra 120a)' Also see Isidore Epstein (ed.), *Babylonian Talmud* (Eng. text), Baba Bathra II, 492–93; and (121a), 498; and Ta'anith (30b), 162.

36 Ṭabarī, *Tārīkh*, I, 585; Qurṭubī, *Jāmiʿ*, XI, 91; Zamakhsharī, Kashshāf, II, 5; Bayḍāwī, *Ta'wīl*, II, 21; Thaʿlabī, *Qiṣaṣ*, 213 (Muqātil, however, says that she was 20 years old: see Thaʿlabī, 215).

37 In other words, '*rūḥanā*' ('Our Spirit') here means Gabriel: Ibn Kathīr, *Tafsīr*, III, 114; Ṭabarī, *Jāmiʿ*, XVI, 60 (also, according to Ibn Isḥāq and Ibn Jurayj); *Jalalayn* (Bayḍāwī margin), II, 20; Qurṭubī, *Jāmiʿ*, XI, 90.

38 Thaʿlabī, *Qiṣaṣ*, 213; Ibn al-Athīr, *Tārīkh*, I, 307–8; Ṭabarī, *Tārīkh*, I, 595–96.

39 Ṭabarī, *Jāmiʿ*, XVI, 59 and *Tārīkh*, I, 599; Ibn al-Athīr, *Tārīkh*, I, 309.

40 For a mystical description of the angel Gabriel (Jibrīl) when he appeared to Mary, see Rūmī, *Mathnawi*, II, 207–12. See Ghurāb, *Tafsīr Ibn ʿArabī*, III, 43 for Ibn ʿArabī's description of the nature of 'spirits' (*al-arwāḥ*) and their ability to materialise and dematerialise as in the case of Gabriel.

41 Qurṭubī, *Jāmiʿ*, VI, 22 (according to Ubayy ibn Kaʿb, Jesus was given some of the 'Spirit' that God used in the creation of Adam).

42 It is generally accepted that the angel Gabriel blew into a hollow (or pit) of the sleeve of Mary's garment: see Qurṭubī, *Jāmiʿ*, XI, 91 (according to Ibn Jurayj and Ibn ʿAbbās); Ibn Kathīr, *Tafsīr*, III, 115-116 (according to 'the trusted scholars') Ṭabarī, *Jāmiʿ*, XVI, 62-63 (on the authority of Wahb); al-Thaʿlabī, *Qiṣaṣ*, 213 (attributed to ʿIkrīma). *Ency. of Islam* (new ed.), 'Mary', 629 adds: 'which she had put off. When the angel had withdrawn, she put on the shirt and became pregnant.' (The source is not mentioned.) Shāh Walī Allāh makes the unusual claim that Gabriel breathed directly into the vulva; see *Prophetic Tales*, trans. Baljon, 55.

43 Ibn al-Athīr, *Tārīkh*, I, 309; Ṭabarī, *Jāmiʿ*, XVI, 62-63; Ibn Kathīr, *Tafsīr*, III, 116 and *Qiṣaṣ*, II, 388-89. Others say that Mary went to her maternal aunt's house, and then this conversation transpired. (Thaʿlabī, *Qiṣaṣ*, 214.) If this account is accepted, then John (عليه السلام) could not have been more than a few months older than Jesus which is in accordance with the Christian claim of six months; see Ṭabarī, *Tārīkh*, I, 585. And John could not have been three years older than Jesus as some have claimed (Suyūṭī, *Itḥāf*, II, 14).

44 Ibn Kathīr, *Qiṣaṣ*, II, 388 and *Tafsīr*, III, 116; Ṭabarī, *Jāmiʿ*, XVI, 64-65. Another story involving Joseph's reaction to Mary's pregnancy appears in some of the literature, in which his doubt becomes dangerous suspicion, and he requires Divine intervention before he accepts the situation: 'It is said that when her paternal cousin, Yūsuf, heard the rumour that she was pregnant from fornication, he feared for her and fled with her, and on the road, he was about to kill her himself when Jibrīl came to him and said it was from the Holy Spirit, so he must not kill her, and thus he desisted'. (Zamakhsharī, *Kashshāf*, III, 5; and Thaʿlabī, *Qiṣaṣ*, 214, who attributes this story to al-Kalbī.)

45 Najjār, *Qiṣaṣ*, 378; Qurṭubī, *Jāmiʿ* I, 93; Thaʿlabī, *Qiṣaṣ*, 215; Ṭabarī, *Jāmiʿ*, XVI, 65; *Jalalayn* (Bayḍāwī margin), II, 20; Badawī, *Batūl*, 35.

46 Ibid., Thaʿlabī; Zamakhsharī, *Kashshāf*, II, 5.

47 Suddī adds that the first pangs were felt while Mary was in her *miḥrāb* in the eastern part of the Temple area. (Ibn Kathīr, *Tafsīr*, III, 116; Ṭabarī, *Jāmiʿ*, XVI, 65.)

48 Ibn Saʿd, *Tabaqāt*, I, 53; Yāqūt, *Muʿjam al-Buldān*, V, 251; Ibn ʿAsākir, *Tārīkh Dimāskh*, I, 22. Also, see Ibn ʿAbd Rabbihi *Ṭabā'iʿ al-Insān*, 106, and *al-ʿIqd al-Farīd*, VII, 256: 'The birthplace of ʿĪsā ibn Maryam is

about three miles from Bayt al-Maqdis.' However, Jabbūr, *Ibn ʿAbd Rabbihi wa ʿIqduhu*, 28–29, describes Ibn ʿAbd Rabbihi as 'more of a poetic historian with some facts interspersed, who makes use of Isrā'īlī or other sources without concern for the chain of authorities.'

49 Ibid.; Yāqūt; Badawī, *Batūl*, 42. He adds that the ruler was taking a census, and as Bethlehem was Joseph's hometown, he took Mary there to be recorded in the census.

50 Ibn Kathīr, *Tafsīr*, III, 116 and *Qiṣaṣ*, II, 390; Ṭabarī, *Jāmiʿ* XVI, 65; Ibn Qutayba, *Maʿārif*, 53; Maqdisī, *Bad'*, III, 121.

51 Suyūṭī, *Itḥāf*, II, 16.

52 The Night Journey (*al-Isrā'*) of the Prophet Muḥammad (ﷺ) and his Ascension (*al-Miʿrāj*) from Jerusalem (Bayt al-Maqdis) to the heavens on the 27th of Rajab. See the beginning of *Ṣaḥīḥ al-Bukhārī* in Ibn Ḥajar, *Fatḥ*.

53 Nasā'ī, *Sunan*, 222, Kitāb aṣ-Ṣalāt; Suyūṭī, *Itḥāf*, II, 16; Ibn Kathīr, *Tafsīr*, III, 116.

54 Ṭabarī rejects the opinion of those who differentiate between the reading of '*m.n*' as '*min*' or '*man*,' i.e., those who read '*min taḥtihā*' as referring to Gabriel, and those who read '*man taḥtahā*' as referring to Jesus, stating that in either case the reference is to Gabriel: Ṭabarī, *Tārīkh*, I, 600; Qurṭubī, *Jāmiʿ*, II, 93 (according to ʿAlqama, aḍ-Ḍaḥḥāk, Qatāda and others); *Jalālayn* (Bayḍāwī margin), II, 20; Thaʿlabī, *Qiṣaṣ*, 215. Badawī, however, prefers the opinion of those who say it is Jesus, stating that it is inconceivable to him that the angel Gabriel would appear under a young woman who was in the process of delivery, and that since it is universally accepted that Jesus spoke from the cradle, then it must have been Jesus who spoke to her from below. (*Batūl*, 48–49.) Others who say it was Jesus are Mujāhid; ʿAbd al-Razzāq on the authority of al-Ḥasan; Saʿīd ibn Jubayr; Ibn Zayd and Ibn Jarīr. (Ibn Kathīr, *Tafsīr*, III, 117.)

55 Zamakhsharī, *Kashshāf*, II, 5; Yāqūt, *Buldān*, I, 521 (attributed to al-Bashsharī).

56 Courtois quotes Arberry's translation of the Sufi al-Kalabādhī's inspiration with reference to Mary's fasting from speech: 'the meaning of fasting is to be absent from the sight of men in the sight of God. For God says in the story of Mary, 'Verily I have vowed to the Merciful One a fast, and I will not speak today with a human being': that is because I am absent from them in the vision of God, and therefore I cannot include in my fast anything that may distract or cut me off from Him.' *Mary in Islam*, 49.

57 Qurṭubī, *Jāmiʿ*, xi, 98; *Ṣaḥīḥ al-Bukhārī* in Ibn Ḥajar, *Fatḥ*, ii, 586, Kitāb al-Aymān wa-Nudhūr, Bāb 31 (no. 6704).

58 Qurṭubī. Similar version attributed to Abū Hurayra in *Ṣaḥīḥ Muslim*, viii, 28, Kitāb al-Ṣiyām.

59 Qurṭubī, *Jāmiʿ*, xi, 98; *Ṣaḥīḥ al-Bukhārī* in Ibn Ḥajar, *Fatḥ*, iv, 116, Kitāb al-Ṣawm, Bāb 8 (no. 1903).

60 Iblīs: the chief devil of the jinns.

61 Thaʿlabī, *Qiṣaṣ*, 213; Ibn Kathīr, *Qiṣaṣ*, ii, 395 (attributed to Ibn Jarīr in his *Tārīkh*); Ibn al-Athīr, *Tārīkh*, i, 306; Ibn Qutayba, *Maʿārif*, 52; Maqdisī, *Bad'*, iii, 121; Suyūṭī, *Faḍā'il*, ii chap. 10, 14. The *qiṣṣa* continues: 'So, he fled to the forest in Jerusalem, and a tree called out to him: "O Prophet of God! This way!" And when he came to it, it was caused to open for him, and he entered its centre, but Iblīs caught a bit of his robe. Then Iblīs informed the tribe that Zakariyyā was there, but they didn't believe him, so he took them there and showed them the piece of Zakariyyā's robe. And they took a cutting tool and struck the tree and split it in half.' These latter elements of the *qiṣṣa* closely resemble a Talmudic story about Isaiah and Manasseh, see H.F.D Sparks (ed.) *Apocryphal O.T.*, 775: 'A tradition that Isaiah was "sawn in two" by Manasseh was known by both Jews and Christians.'

62 For an affirmation of the severity of such an offence in the eyes of Banū Isrā'īl, see *Babylonian Talmud*, Epstein (ed.), Sanhedrin i (50b), 339: 'And the daughter of any priest, if she profane herself by playing the whore, she profaneth her father; she shall be burnt by fire. (Lev. 21:9).'

63 Ibn Kathīr, *Tafsīr*, iii, 118; Ṭabarī, *Jāmiʿ*, xvi, 77; Qurṭubī, *Jāmiʿ*, xi, 100; Dhahabī, *Tārīkh*, i, 570; Ibn al-Athīr, *Tārīkh*, i, 311; For characteristics of the ancient Marys, see *Encycl. Judaica*, xii: There was Miriam, the sister of Aaron and Moses, who was given the title 'prophetess' (p. 82), and in 'Micah with Moses and Aaron as one of the three who led Israel out of Egypt' (p. 83), and for whom 'God intervened.' 'He honoured her by Himself officiating as the kohen to declare her definitely a leper and subsequently to declare her cleansed (Zev. 102a). Because she had waited for Moses by the river, the Israelites waited for her to recover (Sot. 11a) A miraculous well, created during the twilight on the eve of the first Sabbath (Avot. 5:6), accompanied the Children of Israel in the desert due to her merits (Ta'an. 9a). Like Moses and Aaron, she too died by the kiss of God since the angel of death had no power over her. (BB 171)' Another famous Miriam is 'identified with Azubah, the wife of Caleb (I Chron.

2:18). Also, some rabbis hold that even King David was descended from her (Sif. Num.78; Ex. R. 48:34),' (p. 84).

64 Najrān (Negrana) is located in northern Yemen.

65 Muslim, *Ṣaḥīḥ*, XIV,.116-17, Kitāb al-Adab, Bāb bayān mā yustaḥabbu min al-asmā'; Qurṭubī, *Jāmiᶜ*, XI, 100; Dhahabī, *Tārīkh*, I, 570; Ibn al-Athīr, *Tārīkh*, I, 311. Also see Ghurāb, *Tafsīr Ibn ᶜArabī*, III, 47: 'The intention [. . .] is that Mary is his [Hārūn's] sister in religion and genealogical descent.' Ibn ᶜArabī cites two additional similar Qur'ānic statements, one referring to the Arab prophet Ṣāliḥ and the tribe of Thamūd, and the other to the Arab prophet Shuᶜayb and the tribe of Madyan (Midian). The location of the people of Thamūd was probably eastern and central Asia, perhaps in the area of Petra, prior to the Nabateans. (*Shorter Encycl. of Islam*, p. 592.) 'The Midianites were of Arab race, though as neighbours of the Canaanites, they probably intermixed with them.' They were nomads whose territory in the time of Moses was N.E. Sinai. (Yūsuf ᶜAlī, trans., *Holy Qur'an*, p. 364, note.)

66 Zamakhsharī, *Kashshāf*, II, 6.

67 Badawī, *Batūl*, 60.

68 Thaᶜlabī, *Qiṣaṣ*, 216.

69 Ibid.; Ṭabarī, *Tārīkh*, I, 605; *New Columbia Encycl.*, 1233. Herod, the Great was the son of Antipater II and was friendly with Marc Antony, who got him the title of King of Judea.

70 Ibid., Ṭabarī; Thaᶜlabī, *Qiṣaṣ*, 216

71 Qurṭubī, *Jāmiᶜ*, XII, 126; Ṭabarī, *Jāmiᶜ*, VIII, 25-26; Ibn Kathīr, *Tafsīr*, III, 246. (Both Ibn Kathīr and Qurṭubī attribute the choice of Ramla to Abū Hurayra.) Yāqūt, *Buldān*, 69-70: 'Ramla is 18 days [on foot] from Bayt al-Maqdis.'

72 Ibid.; Qurṭubī; Ibn Kathīr; Ṭabarī.

73 Ibn Kathīr, *Tafsīr*, III,.246; Maqdisī, *Bad'*, III, 120.

74 Suyūṭī, *Itḥāf*, II, 166.

75 Yaqūt, *Buldān*, II, 166.

76 *Synaxaire*, Patrol, Or., XVI, 407-410. Cairo ed., II, 154-55 (Maqrīzī, *Athār*, 193, II, 101).

77 Badawī, *Batūl*, 76.

78 See Hennecke-Schneemelcher, *N. T. Apocrypha*, I, 409, for the account of this incident from the Arabic Infancy Gospel.

79 Maqrīzī, *Athār*, 101-2; Yāqūt, *Buldān*, III, 245 (for location of Samannūd).

80 Badawī, *Batūl*, 76-79; Meinardus, *Holy Family*, 19.

81 The *Shām* previously described the northern part of the ancient Arabian peninsula, including Palestine. The largest part of the ancient *Shām* would be the contemporary Republic of Syria. The adjectival form '*shāmī*' is still used in this greater sense. Nowadays, however, the *Shām* usually refers to Syria or its capital city Damascus.

82 Thaʿlabī, *Qiṣaṣ*, 219.

83 Ṭabarī, *Tārīkh*, I, 585; Badawī, *Batūl*, 151.

84 Ibn al-Athīr, *Tārīkh*, I, 320; Thaʿlabī, *Qiṣaṣ*, 225-226 (Attributed to Qatāda and Muqātil, who add: 'And God knows best' (*wa Allāhu aʿlam*)).

85 Thaʿlabī records the name as Shamʿūn al-Ṣafār; assumedly the reference is to Samʿān al-Ṣafā (Simon Cephas, i.e., Peter), see Gibson, *Apocry. Sinaitica*, 56 (Arabic); 52 (English).

86 This appears to be a symbolic reference to the Mārūt of ancient Babylon mentioned in the Qur'ān (2:102). If understood according to Yūsuf ʿAlī's commentary (which is based on Bayḍāwī and others), 'The word "angel" as applied to Hārūt and Mārūt is figurative. It means good men, of knowledge, science (or wisdom) and power,' 45 note. By extension, in the above text Mārūt could mean a king with those characteristics, or if taken literally, it could refer to the same 'angelic' Mārūt, who reappears in the time of Jesus.

87 Thaʿlabī, *Qiṣaṣ*, 227. Waddy, *Women*, 37, includes a reference to the assertion that Mary spent her last years in what is now modern Turkey: 'Turkey treasures the home where the Virgin is said to have lived in her old age. Tradition [*qiṣaṣ*] says that St. John, instructed by Jesus to care for his mother, took her in later years to Ephesus. On a wooded mountainside above the ruins of the ancient city, the traces of a first century house have been found, and round them a small church has been built. The place itself was only discovered a hundred years ago, through the dream of a German nun. But the tradition [*qiṣaṣ*] that the Virgin lived in some such spot in this area is a very early one [. . .] Muslims honour it, and by the altar are written passages from the Gospels, the Muslim traditions [*ḥadīth*] and the Qur'ān, in praise of the Mother of Jesus.'

88 Ibn al-Athīr, *Tārīkh*, I, 320.

89 Ibn Hishām, *Sīra*, IV, 188 (attributed to Ibn Isḥāq).

90 Hennecke-Schneemelcher, *N.T. Apocrypha*, I, 444-81; and Hone, trans., *Apocryphal N.T.*, 63-91 for the full text of the Gospel of Nicodemus. Also see James, *Apocryphal N.T.*, 228-70 for the full text of the Acts of John the Apostle, which describe his activities in Ephesus, with no mention of Mary—dated no later than mid-second century. Also *New Columbia Encycl.*, 2189; 2234. Also Hennecke-Schneemelcher, *N.T. Apocrypha*, I, 418, for further references to the Apocryphal literature about Mary, and 429 for references about Mary's death.

91 Suyūṭī, *Itḥāf*, II, chap. 10, p. 14. Also see Ibn Baṭṭūṭa, *Tuḥfa*, 46, in which he attributes this account to Isrā'īlī sources: 'At the bottom of the said Valley of Jahannum (the Valley of Gehenna or Hinnom: II Kings 23:10) is a church which the Christians venerate, for here, they say, is the Tomb of Mary—Peace be upon her!'

92 Ibn ʿAsākir, *Tārīkh*, I, 264.

93 Qurṭubī, *Jāmiʿ*, IV, 84; Badawī, *Batūl*, 28; 151.

94 *Ṣiddīq*, sometimes translated as 'righteous' or 'upright' has a broader and deeper meaning in Arabic (see: chap. 5).

95 Maqdisī (*Bad'* III, 123) does not clarify which Umayya this is. In *Tārīkh Dimshq*, Ibn ʿAsākir describes several Umayyas; however the only poet amongst them is Umayya ibn Abī al-Ṣalt, the well-known 'pre-Islamic' poet and contemporary of the Prophet Muḥammad (ﷺ). It is interesting to note that although Umayya ibn Abī al-Ṣalt did not die a Muslim, according to the data presented by Ibn ʿAsākir, Umayya struggled with the issue of believing in the truth of Muḥammad (ﷺ) and his message (118ff.), and at one point (123), 'He almost accepted Islam'; and in another incident (130) when the Prophet (ﷺ) recites the Chapter of Yāsīn and Umayya is asked what he has to say about it, he states: 'I bear witness that he [Muḥammad ﷺ] is following the truth.' But after the early Battle of Badr (624), Umayya leaves Islam (130), and according to Hitti, *History* (108), 624 was the year in which Umayya died. Thus, if Ibn ʿAsākir's account is truly representative of Umayya ibn Abī al-Ṣalt's character, one cannot rule out the possibility that he could have been the author of the above poem about Mary.

96 *Dīn*: religion

97 *Subḥanallāh*: Glorified/Transcendent is God.

98 The ʿĀd are frequently mentioned together with the Thamūd in the Qur'ān. According to Yūsuf ʿAlī, the story of the ʿĀd people 'belongs to Arabian tradition [. . .] They occupied a large tract of country in

Southern Arabia, from ʿUmmān at the mouth of the Persian Gulf to Ḥadhramaut and Yemen at the southern end of the Red Sea,' (trans., *Holy Qur'ān*, 358, note. *The Encycl. of Islam* reiterates the Qur'anic statement that the ʿĀd, to whom the prophet Hūd was sent, were an ancient and mighty tribe that lived directly after the time of Noah (7:69; 41:15). However, the author rejects the possibility of a definitive location for the habitat of these ancient people. (The same article appears in both the shorter (13) and the new edition (I, 169).

99 The reference is probably to the Banū Jurhām, who took over custody of the Kaʿba after the descendents of Ishmael, the son of Abraham, according to Ibn Hishām, *Sīra*, I, 102-4; Ibn Kathīr, *Sīra*, , 57; Hitti, *History*, 57.

100 Maqdisī, *Bad'*, 123-124. My translation of this poem was re-cast into poetic form by S.A. Schleifer.

101 See chap. I for a discussion of Qur'ān 19:27-28 about the aspersion, 'O sister of Aaron' and Mary's public display of the infant Jesus. In addition, according to popular Muslim belief, this intense dedication of Mary to Jesus and his mission, both emotionally and doctrinally, continued until her death.

102 Maqrīzī, *Āthār*, 101-102; Badawī, *Batūl*, 76-79.

103 See Netton, *Allah Transcendent*, for a semiotic interpretation of Islamic symbolism.

104 Although references to parents normally include both father and mother, and thereby require additional Qur'ānic statements or ḥadīth clarification when the intention is for mothers only, in the case of Mary and Jesus, all such references would be applied to her, as Jesus had no father.

105 Qurṭubī, *Jāmiʿ*, II, 13; Ibn Kathir, *Tafsīr*, I, 119.

106 Ibid.; and Ṭabarī, *Jāmiʿ*, I, 390.

107 *Ṣaḥiḥ al-Bukhārī* in Ibn Ḥajar, *Fatḥ*, X, 401, Kitāb al-Adab, Bāb 2, no. 5971; Ṣiddīq Khān, *Ḥusn al-uswa*, Bāb mā warada fī birr al-wālida, 235.

108 Ibn Ḥajar, *Fatḥ*, X, 403.

109 See Shawkānī's discussion of *jihād* in the following footnote.

110 The chain of authorities (*isnād*) and text are from *Ṣaḥīḥ al-Bukhārī* in Ibn Ḥajar, *Fatḥ*, VI, 33, Kitāb al-Jihād, Bāb 22 no. 2818. Also see Shawkānī, *Nayl al-Awṭār*, IX, 72; Shawkānī defines *jihād* as (1) the killing of non-believers (*al-kuffār*) when legally justified and (2) the struggle against the *nafs* (soul/ego) and *al-shayṭān* (Satan) and corruption by: first the hand (i.e. actively); then if that is not possible, the tongue, and finally

with the heart. He further states that *jihād* against the *kuffār* was *farḍ ʿayn* (obligatory for each male Muslim) during the time of the Prophet (ﷺ) at specific times when he designated it to be so, and *farḍ ʿayn* if so designated by the *imām* (caliph), but it is basically *farḍ kifāya* (obligatory upon a group within the Muslim community, not for each individual). Ibn Ḥajar confirms that *jihād* is *farḍ kifāya, Fatḥ*, VI, 17.

111 The chain of authorities and the text are from *Ṣaḥīḥ Muslim*, XVI, 103-4, Kitāb al-birr wa'ṣila wa'l-ādāb, Bāb al-wālidayn wa annahumā aḥaqq bihi; Ṣiddīq Khān, *Ḥusn al-uswa*, 23, Bāb mā warada fī birr al-wālida; al-Shawkānī, *Nayl*, IX, 83-84. A subsequent ḥadīth in Kitāb al-birr wa'ṣila wa'l-ādāb of *Ṣaḥiḥ Muslim* makes it clear that the reference is to either or both parents. On the authority of ʿAmr ibn al-ʿĀṣ, in response to a request to participate in *jihād*, the Prophet (ﷺ) asked: 'Is one of your parents alive?' XVI, 104.

112 The meaning is that it could have been *farḍ ʿayn* (see above footnote) if so indicated by the Prophet (ﷺ) or the caliphs, as a special dispensation, but that it is definitely not the general case.

113 The *nafs*: the soul/self. The stage in which one is struggling with egotistical and worldly concerns which conflict with one's attempt to purify the soul and attain to God on a spiritual level is '*al-nafs al-ammāra bi'l-sū*" (the soul commanding to evil) [12:53]. This stage 'forms the starting point for the Sufi way of purification;' see Schimmel, *Mystical Dimensions*, 112. For al-Ghazālī's discussion of the stages of the *nafs* see *Iḥyā'*, III, 4-6, Kitāb 'Ajā'ib al-qalb, Bayān maʿnā al-nafs wa'l-rūḥ wa'l-qalb wa'l-ʿaql; III, 215-44 (Kitāb dhamm al-dunyā.)

114 al-Shawkānī, *Nayl*, IX, 84-85.

115 Ibid., 84; Ṣiddīq Khān, *Ḥusn al-uswa*, 236.

116 Abdul Razack and Abdul Jawad al-Banna, *Women and the Family*, 15.

117 *Ṣaḥīḥ al-Bukhārī*, in Ibn Ḥajar, *Fatḥ*, VI, 47. Kitāb al-jihād wa al-siyar, Bāb 16, no. 2840. In Ibn Ḥajar's discussion on p. 48, he states that '*al-kharīfa*' means one year, and he quotes Qurṭubī as stating that the mention of 70 is because of the desire to indicate 'a very great number,' i.e., far away from Hell, not the precise number of seventy. He adds that this ḥadīth is found in other collections: Nasā'ī, on the authority of ʿUqba ibn Āmir; Ṭabarānī, on the authority of ʿAmr ibn ʿAbasa; and Abū Yaʿlā, on the authority of ʿMuʿādh ibn Anas, and in all these accounts the number of years stated is 100.

118 *Ṣaḥīḥ al-Bukhārī* in Ibn Ḥajar, *Fatḥ*, v, 146, Kitāb al-ʿItq, Bāb 1, no. 2517.

119 *Ṣaḥiḥ al-Bukhārī* in Ibn Ḥajar, *Fatḥ*, x, 426, Kitāb al-Adab, Bāb 18, no. 5995; Ṣiddīq Khān, *Ḥusn al-uswa*, Bāb mā warada fi birr al-awlād wa'l-aqārib, 237-38.

120 Ibn Kathīr, *Tafsīr*, I, 363. Also, see Ghurāb, *Tafsīr Ibn ʿArabī*, I, 363, III, 449.

121 Ibid., Ibn Kathīr, III, 119 and *Qiṣaṣ*, II, 396.

122 Badawī, *Batūl*, 84; Ṭabarī, *Tārīkh*, I, 597-98; Thaʿlabī, *Qiṣaṣ*, 217; Ibn al-Athīr, *Tārīkh*, I, 313. A similar account is found in Netton, *Ikhwān aṣ-Ṣafā*, 49, and in the Talmud; see Epstein (ed.), *Babylonian Talmud* (Eng. text). (Sanhedrin II (91 a-b), 610-11), but the differences are notable. Besides the fact that the above account emphasises the importance of Mary's relationship with her son and his miraculous powers, it does not stress the 'Judeo-Christian' ethic of forgiveness as Netton suggests on p. 50 with reference to the Ikhwān account, as wanton theft is a serious crime in Islam, especially from one who has shown you charity. The Talmudic account is also presented for a completely different purpose, which is to show 'figuratively' that the two essences, 'body' and 'soul' can use each other to escape blame for an evil, sinful deed.

123 Ibid., Badawī, Ṭabarī; Thaʿlabī; Ibn al-Athīr.

124 Maqrīzī, *Athār*, II, 101-2 for reference to this particular period of exile.

125 Badawī, *Batūl*, 84.

126 *walī/waliyya*: the beloved (by God), the friend (of God), the victorious (for God); a saintly, holy man or woman.

127 Smith, *Rābiʿa*, 1, For the original, see Shabistarī, *Rosenflor des Geheimnisses (Gulshan-i Raz)* (Persian and German texts), p. 11 in the German text.

128 Smith, *Rābiʿa*, 2.

129 *Ṣaḥīḥ Muslim*, XVII, 69., Kitāb al-tawba, Bāb saʿat raḥmat Allāh taʿāla wa annahā taghlib ghaḍabahu.

130 The Muslim mother's role is also considered a contributing factor to the equilibrium of the family unit and of society , see Fatima Heeren's discussion of the Islamic approach to family life: Lemu and Heeren, *Woman in Islam*, 34-35.

131 Ibn Kathīr, *Tafsīr*, I, 359-60.

132 Ṭabarī, *Jāmiʿ*, III, 234.

133 Ibn Kathīr, *Tafsīr*, I, 363; 3, 114.

134 al-Qurṭubī, *Jāmiʿ*, IV, 84-85; XVIII, 204.

135 In the following interpretations of the Qur'ān, the phrase '*maʿa ar-rākiʿīn*' is translated as 'with' them: *The Holy Qur'ān*, Yūsuf ʿAlī, trans.; *The Glorious Koran*, Marmaduke Pickthall, trans.; *The Message of the Qur'an*, Muḥammad Asad, trans.; *The Koran*, N.J. Dawood, trans.; *The Koran*, George Sale, trans. However, in Arthur J. Arberry's translation, *The Koran Interpreted*, he does not give a literal rendering of 3:43, and in his paraphrase, he omits the preposition entirely: 'Mary, be obedient to thy Lord, prostrating and bowing before Him.'

136 Qurṭubī, *Jāmiʿ*, IV, 85.

137 Zamakhsharī, *Kashshāf*, I, 144.

138 *Babylonian Talmud*, Epstein (ed.), Sanhedrin I (60b-61a), 412, cf (1); 413, cf (3); 414; *Encycl. Biblica*, III, 3824-25; *Jewish Encycl.*, X, 166; *Encycl. of Religion*, X, 194; *New Schaff-Herzog Encycl. of Rel.*, IX, 154; Baron, *A Social and Religious History of the Jews*, I, 350-51, cf (28).

139 Mawdūdī, *Tafsīr Sūrat al-Kahf wa Maryam*, I, 87.

140 Ibn Kathīr, *Tafsīr*, IV, 394.

141 According to Islam, when the prophet Abraham (عليه السلام) left his wife Hājar (Hagar) and her babe in the desolate area where the Holy Sanctuary of Makka now stands, in desperation she paced back and forth between the two hills, al-Ṣafā and al-Marwa, beseeching her Lord for help. In answer to her prayer the water of Zamzam sprang forth. (Ibn Kathīr, *Sīra*, I, 56.) In both the greater and the lesser pilgrimages in Islam, Muslims commemorate Hagar's experience by offering prayers while walking between al-Ṣafā and al-Marwa, and upon drinking from the well of Zamzam.

142 Mawdūdī, *Tafsīr*, I, 89. Mawdūdī's statement that Mary's words 'could not have been' the result of the pain of childbirth is in keeping with the image of Mary which rejects any physical uncleanness or other imperfection as an attribute of her. See Rāzī, *Mafātīḥ*, II, 467, and Qurṭubī, *Jāmiʿ*, IV, 71, and chap. 4 of this study, for a general discussion of this point.

143 *Ṣaḥīḥ al-Bukhārī*, in Ibn Ḥajar, *Fatḥ*, XIII, 220, Kitāb al-Tamannī, Bāb 6, no. 7234, Nasā'ī, *Sunan*, IV, 2, Kitāb al-Janā'iz, Bāb Tamannī al-Mawt (on the authority of Abū Hurayra).

144 Ibn Ḥajar, *Fatḥ*, XIII, 221.

145 Aḥmad ibn Ḥanbal, *Musnad*, II, 316 (from a longer ḥadīth: Qurṭubī, *Jāmiᶜ* XI, 92).

146 *Ṣaḥīḥ Muslim*, XVII, 7, Kitāb al-Dhikr wa'l-Duᶜā' wa'l-Tawba wa'l-Istighfār, Bāb karāha tamannī al-mawt li ḍurr nazala bihi; *Ṣaḥīḥ al-Bukhārī*, in Ibn Ḥajar, *Fatḥ*, X, 127, Kitāb al-Maraḍ, Bāb 19, no. 5671 and VIII, 242, no. 362; Abū Dāwūd, *Sunan*, III, 188, Karāhiyya tamannī al-mawt; (a similar version is found in Nasā'ī, *Sunan*, IV, p 3-4, Kitāb al-Janā'iz, al-Du'ā' bi'l- mawt; Qurṭubī, *Jāmiᶜ*, XI, 92.)

147 Nawawī on *Ṣaḥīḥ Muslim*, XVII, 7-8.

148 Qurṭubī, *Jāmiᶜ*, XI, 92.

149 Ghurāb, *Tafsīr Ibn ᶜArabī*, III, 46.

150 Qurṭubī, *Jāmiᶜ*, XI, 92.

151 Some commentators say that it was customary at that time to fast from speech as well as from food for a day. See Ṭabarī, *Jāmiᶜ*, XVI, 75. *The New Schaff-Herzog Encycl. of Rel.*, IV, 281 mentions that fasting as an act of self-abnegation and humility occurred (1 Kings 21:28 and Jer. 14:12), and that the usual period of abstention was one day (1 Sam. 24:14). As details are not mentioned, however, it is not clear whether these fasts included abstaining from speech as well as food; thus this may have been an additional requirement made specifically for Mary in her particular circumstance.

152 Ṭabarī, *Jāmiᶜ*, VI, 315.

153 Qurṭubī, *Jāmiᶜ*, VI, 251; XVIII, 203.

154 Rūzbihān al-Baqlī, *ᶜArā'is*, II, 333.

155 Ibid., I, 80.

156 Suyūṭī, *Itḥāf*, I, chap. 7, 196; al-ᶜUlaymī, *al-Uns*, II, 369-70.

157 Badawī, *Batūl*, 112.

158 Qurṭubī, *Jāmiᶜ*, IV, 82. Also see Mujāhid, *Tafsīr*, I, 127: 'God made you [Mary] good of faith.'

159 Ibid.; Qurṭubī.

160 Khāzin, *Tafsīr*, I, 228. Also see Rūzbihān, *ᶜArā'is*, I, 83.

161 Ṭabarī, *Jamiᶜ* III, 262; Muqātil, *Tafsīr*, 168.

162 al-Razī, *Tafsīr*, II, 467, The Qur'anic reference is to 19:29-32.

163 Qushayrī, *Laṭā'if*, I, 249, 254.

164 Qurṭubī, *Jāmiᶜ*, IV, 82.

165 Ibn Kathīr, *Tafsīr*, III, 194.

166 The chain of authorities and the text are from *Ṣaḥīḥ al-Bukhārī* in Ibn Ḥajar, *Fatḥ*, VI, 470, Kitāb al-Anbiyā, Bāb 45 (no. 3432); *Ṣaḥīḥ Muslim*, XV, 197-98, Kitāb al-Faḍā'il, Bāb Faḍā'il Khadīja; al-Dhahabī, *Siyar*, II, 83; Qurṭubī, *Jamiᶜ*, IV, 83; Ṭabarī, *Jāmiᶜ*, III, 263; Ibn Kathīr, *Tafsīr*, IV, 394 (this version includes Fāṭima and Āsiya (ﷺ), as well, on the authority of Ibn ᶜAbbās.)

167 Ṭabarī, *Jāmiᶜ*, III, 266: (Ṭabarī quotes al-Qāsim to the effect that the reference is to the nations of her time).

168 Ibid., 264; Ibn Ḥusām ad-Dīn, *Kanz*, XII, 132, Bāb fī Faḍā'il Ahl al-Bayt (no. 34347).

169 See discussion below of 'Women who ride camels.'

170 Dhahabī, *Siyar*, II, 95; Ibn Ḥusām ad-Dīn, *Kanz*, XII, 109 (no. 34224) (al-Ḥākim, on the authority of Abū Saᶜīd); *Ṣaḥīḥ al-Bukhārī* in Ibn Ḥajar, *Fatḥ*, VII, 105 (no. 3767): (Bukhārī alludes to this ḥadīth by his chapter heading and inclusion of a full *isnād*. Ibn Ḥajar affirms that the full version found in al-Ḥākim's collection has a strong, cohesive *isnād*); Ibn Saᶜd, *Ṭabaqāt*, II, 248.

171 Dhahabī, *Siyar*, II, 86, Ibn Kathīr, *Qiṣaṣ*, II, 376-377: Ibn ᶜAsākir, on the authority of Ibn ᶜAbbās.

172 Ibn Kathīr, *Qiṣaṣ*, II, 378-379; Also see Qurṭubī, *Jāmiᶜ*, IV, 8, who includes the same ranking order based on another version of the ḥadīth transmitted by Mūsā ibn ᶜUqba with his *isnād*, on the authority of Ibn ᶜAbbās, which Qurṭubī classifies as *ḥasan* ('good').

173 Ibn Kathīr, *Qiṣaṣ*, II, 381.

174 Ibid., 381. (In another manuscript, instead of '*anba'anā*' is found '*ḥaddathanā*').

175 Ibn Kathīr, *Qiṣaṣ*, II, 382; al-Wāsiṭī, *Faḍā'il*, 67-68.

176 al-Wāsiṭī, *Faḍā'il*, 68: see footnote to this account.

177 I.e., non-Muslim sources, primarily Jewish and Christian, which may or not have a basis in the Qur'ān or Sunna of the Prophet (ﷺ).

178 Ibn Kathīr, *Qiṣaṣ*, II, 383.

179 See Ibn Kathīr, *Tafsīr*, v.I, 362-63 for a ḥadīth compiled by al-Tirmidhī, on the authority of Anas which includes the most esteemed women of all nations, beginning with Mary, then Khadīja, Fāṭima and Āsiya. Ibn Kathīr says this ḥadīth is reported singly by Tirmidhī, and he considers it sound.

180 Ṭabarī, *Jāmiᶜ*, XVI, 62.

181 Ibn Manẓūr, *Lisān*, XI, 42.

182 Ibid., XI, 43.

183 Khāzin, *Tafsīr*, I, 224. Also, Ibn Manẓūr, *Lisān*, XI, 43: '*Batūl*' in the phrase, 'the *batūl* of female creation' has been generalised to mean the woman who is separated from other women because of her beauty and spirituality; thus, Fāṭima bint Muḥammad has been called 'the *Batūl*,' while the phrase containing another form of the word, 'the *mubattala* of created beings' may refer to any woman whose combination of beautiful features are perfectly matched.

184 Ibn Kathīr, *Qiṣaṣ*, II, 388.

185 The reference here is to a genre of writings which describe the merits (*faḍā'il*) of the city of Jerusalem.

186 Ibn al-Jawzī, *Faḍā'il*, 97-98. A similar version with the same chain of authorities is found in al-Wāsiṭī, *Faḍā'il*, 45.

187 *Ṣaḥīḥ Muslim*, IX, 174-75, Kitāb al-Nikāḥ, Bāb istiḥbāb al-nikāḥ li-man ṭāqat nafsuhu wa wajada mu'na; *Ṣaḥiḥ al-Bukhārī* in Ibn Ḥajar, *Fatḥ*, IX, 112, Kitāb al-Nikāḥ, Bab 2 (no. 5066). Also see *Muʿjam Lārūs*, 1274: '*al-wijā*'' is the container which a woman uses for the cleansing of blood. Thus the use of the word '*al-wijā*'', is a reminder of both the cleansing aspect of fasting and, its consequent protection of the virgin from the fornicator.

188 See 2:228-37 and 65:1-7 for the various conditions of widowhood and divorce, all of which allow the woman to remarry. Also, for the legal rulings in details of the ʿ*idda* (the waiting period before remarriage), see Marghinānī, *Hidāya*, II, Bāb al-ʿidda.

189 *Ṣaḥīḥ Muslim*, VIII, 68, Kitāb al-iʿtikāf. see 66, where Nawawī defines the *iʿtikāf* as the living of an individual in the mosque in isolation from society for the special purpose of worship, and on p. 69, Nawawī says that it is generally accepted that the *iʿtikāf* must be practised in the mosque by any man who desires to do so, but Abū Ḥanīfa says that for a woman it should be done in the place where she usually prays in her home; and on 67, Nawawī states that the *iʿtikāf* is *mustaḥabb* (legally allowed), but it is not legally required for a Muslim, even during the last ten days of Ramaḍān. And the obligation of the Muslim to fast the month of Ramaḍān does not contain the *sharṭ* (condition) that he practise the *iʿtikāf*, rather that the *iʿtikāf* may be practised either for a limited period of days or for an hour or less. Nawawī adds that it has to be, however, by intention (*niyya*), and if the

person leaves, and then returns, he must state his intention (*niyya*) again. Also, *Ṣaḥīḥ al-Bukhārī* in Ibn Ḥajar, *Fatḥ*, IV, 271, Kitāb al-Iʿtikāf, Bāb 1 (no. 2026); and for ḥadīths about the performing of the *iʿtikāf* at times other than Ramaḍān, see 283, Bāb 14, and pp. 284-85, Bāb 15-16.

190 *Ṣaḥīḥ Muslim*, IX, 175-76, Kitāb al-Nikāḥ; Aḥmad ibn Ḥanbal, *Musnad*, III, 241; 259; 285.

191 *Ṣaḥīḥ Muslim*, IX, 177. See 176, where Nawawī comments that according to the scholars (*ʿulamāʾ*), '*at-tabattul*' is the cutting off of relations with the opposite sex and permanently rejecting marriage for the worship of God. And among the examples of this is Mary the *Batūl*. He also includes Fāṭima the *batūl* because of her distinction amongst the women of her time in terms of religious excellence. (But Fāṭima was not the *batūl* in the sense that Mary was, the most obvious difference being that Fāṭima married ʿAlī and had children by him.) Nawawī, commenting on the mention of castration in the ḥadīth, clarifies that this is a figure of speech, meaning that they would have severed relations with women and other attractions of this world, as the actual castration of human beings is forbidden (*ḥarām*).

192 Ibn al-Qayyim seems to be referring to the relationship between the specific nature of the first five *āyāt* of the Chapter of Taḥrīm, the generalisation of the specific in *āyāt* 6-7, and the provision of models in 10-12 as examples of the point made in the preceding *āyāt*.

193 The reference here is: (1) to the innocent but damaging behaviour of ʿĀʾisha which made possible the false accusations against her and Ṣafwān ibn Muʿaṭṭal al-Musallamī, made by Miṣṭa, a relative of Abū Bakr al-Ṣiddīq, and by Ḥamna, the sister of one of the wives of the Prophet, Zaynab bint Jaḥsh. The incident, which is described in a very long ḥadīth runs as follows: ʿĀʾisha had accompanied the Prophet (ﷺ) on a military expedition. After the battle, upon hearing the order to return to al-Madīna, she realised that her necklace had broken at a site just outside of the encampment, and she went to look for the pieces. By the time she returned, the army had left, thinking that she was with them inside her covered litter. She waited in her place assuming that they would soon discover that she was missing and return for her; eventually, she fell asleep. Ṣafwān ibn Muʿaṭṭal also remained behind as he had fallen asleep earlier and missed the departure of the army. While walking about late at night, he discovered ʿĀʾisha sleeping. With the innocence of youth, she mounted his camel without conversation, and he led it forward to the site

where the army had stopped to rest. The evil slander that ensued caused personal and community problems to the degree that the major tribes of Aws and Khazraj almost came to blows. The matter was definitively concluded in ʿĀ'isha's favour with the revelation of Qur'ān 12:18 which speaks of the prophet Joseph's (ﷺ) innocence in the face of similar false accusations: see *Ṣaḥīḥ Muslim*, XVII, 102-14, Kitāb at-Tawba, Bāb fī ḥadīth al ifk wa qabūl tawbat al-qādhif for the complete account; and (2)Ḥafsa, the wife of the Prophet, and her disclosure of his confidence; see Qur'ān 66:3, and Yūsuf ʿAlī's comments: *Holy Qur'ān*, 1569 note.

194 Ibn al-Qayyim, *Tafsīr*, 497.

195 Ibid.

196 The masculine form '*al-ṣiddīq*,' minus '*al-akbar*' is the title given to Abū Bakr, the first of the Four Righteous Caliphs.

197 The masculine form '*al-muṣṭafā*' is one of the titles of the Prophet Muḥammad (ﷺ).

198 Ibn al-Qayyim, *Tafsīr*, 497-98.

199 Qurṭubī, *Jāmiʿ*, XII, 172-73.

200 Dhahabī, *Siyar*, II, 134. Dhahabī states that al-Ḥākim confirms this ḥadīth as sound.

201 Ibid., II, 92; Khāzin, *Tafsīr*, IV, 299 (on the authority of Anas ibn Mālik; and Tirmidhī said it is a sound ḥadīth (*ṣaḥīḥ*); Rāzī, *Tafsīr*, II, 468; Thaʿlabī, *Qiṣaṣ*, 208 (a slightly different version, in which the order of mention is Mary, Āsiya, Khadīja, Fāṭima; on the authority of Abū Hurayra).

202 Rāzī, *Tafsīr*, II, 468.

203 Qurṭubī, *Jāmiʿ*, IV, 83.

204 Rūzbihān al-Baqlī, *ʿArā'is*, I, 80.

205 Ibn Manẓūr, *Lisān*, X, 193: '*al-ṣiddīq* is the grammatical form of *mubālagha* (intensification of the basic meaning) of *ṣidq* (truth, sincerity, correctness). It means the steadfast in being trustworthy, truthful, sincere of faith and belief, the one whose word is made credible by his deed.' The first example Ibn Manẓūr provides is Qur'ān 5:75, stating that the meaning is that Mary is the possessor of these characteristics.

206 See chap. 1 of this study in the discussion of the site of Jesus's birth for the refence to the *Isrā' wa'l-Miʿrāj*.'

207 al-Wāsiṭī, *Faḍā'il*, 49; Ibn al-Jawzī, *Faḍā'il*, 121, cf 35: al-Walīd (d.193 AH) was a student of al-ʿUzā'ī. See chap. 1 of this study for a discussion of the site of Mary's grave.

208 *walī/waliyya*: a friend [of God]; popularly expressed as 'saint'.

209 See the Chapter of Mary (19:51 and 54) for references to both Moses and Ishmael (﵇) as combined messenger and prophet, while, for example, Aaron and Idrīs (﵇) are described as prophets only (19:53 and 56). Some commentators have identified Idrīs with the Biblical Enoch, who walked with God (Gen. v.21–24): see Yūsuf ʿAli, trans., *Holy Qur'an*, 779, note.

210 See al-Ḥallāj, *Tawāsīn* (commentary by Rūzbihān al-Baqlī), 160, cf 2 for discussion of the question of whether or not there exists a historical distinction between the classification of prophet and messenger with reference to the Prophet and Messenger Muḥammad (ﷺ).

211 Suyūṭī, *Faḍā'il*, II, chap. 12, 88. Also see al-Kalbī's statement in rejection of prophethood for Mary: Qurṭubī, *Jāmiʿ*, IV, 83.

212 *al-ijmāʿ = al-jamāʿa*

213 Bayḍāwī, I, 115.

214 Yūsuf ʿAlī, trans., *The Holy Qur'an*, 590, note.

215 Ṭabarī, *Jāmiʿ*, III, 262.

216 The Quraysh were the tribe of the Prophet Muḥammad (ﷺ).

217 *Ṣaḥīḥ al-Bukhārī* in Ibn Ḥajar, *Fatḥ*, VI, 473 Kitāb al-Anbiyā', Bāb 46 (no. 3434); Ṭabarī, *Jāmiʿ*, III, 262; Ibn Kathīr, *Tafsīr*, I, 363. Also, this ḥadīth is among the very few ḥadīths of Bukhārī of the category which has been criticised by some of the ḥadīth scholars: see Ṣiddīqi, *Ḥadīth Literature*, 201 (category (e)) 'praise of a particular tribe.'

218 Ṭabarī, *Jāmiʿ*, III, 262.

219 Ibn Ḥajar, *Fatḥ*, VI, 473–474.

220 Ibn Kathīr, *Qiṣaṣ*, II, 374.

221 Ibid.

222 Ibid.

223 See Qur'ān 44:30–33.

224 See Yūsuf ʿAlī, trans., *The Holy Qur'an*, 1349, note.

225 Ibn Kathīr, *Qiṣaṣ*, II, 375.

226 His full name is ʿAlī ibn Ismāʿīl ibn Isḥāq ibn Sālim ibn ʿAbdullāh ibn Mūsā ibn Bilāl ibn Abī Burda al-Ashʿarī, born in Baṣra (d. 324 AH): see *Shorter Encycl. of Islam*, 46.

227 Ibn Kathīr, *Qiṣaṣ*, II, 375.

228 Ibn Kathīr, *Tafsīr*, II, 81.

229 Ibn Manẓūr, *Lisān*, v, 56-57, art. *fiṭra*: 'An innate disposition to the Truth, i.e., that there is no god except God and that God is the Lord of all things and their Creator.' Also Zirr and Durkee, *Shādhdhuliyyah*, I, 9: 'nature, innate character, original nature, primordial nature.'

230 Muslim, *Ṣaḥīḥ*, XVI, 210, Kitāb al-qadr, Bāb kull mawlūd ʿalā al-fiṭra. According to Nawawī, the meaning of '*al-ḥiḍn*' is *al-janb* (the side), but it is also said to mean '*al-khāṣira*' (the hip, waist).

231 Ibid., XV, 119-20, Kitāb al-faḍā'il, Bāb faḍā'il ʿĪsā; *Ṣaḥīḥ al-Bukhārī* in Ibn Ḥajar, *Fatḥ*, VI, 469, Kitāb al-Anbiyā', Bāb 44 (no. 3431); Ibn Ḥanbal, *Musnad*, II, 233; 274-75; 288; 292; 319; 368; Ibn Ḥusām al-Dīn, *Kanz al-ʿUmmāl*, I, 503-4 (nos. 32354 and 32355); Zamakhsharī, *Kashshāf*, I, 142; Qurṭubī, *Jāmiʿ*, IV, 68; Ibn Kathīr, *Tafsīr*, I, 359 and *Qiṣaṣ*, II, 370-71; Ṭabarī, Jāmiʿ, III, 239-40 (Abū Hurayra's narration and those of other narrators); Khāzin, *Tafsīr*, I, 225; *Jalālayn*, I, 113; Thaʿlabī, *Qiṣaṣ*, 208. Ibn al-Athīr elaborates on this ḥadīth with the following account: 'Idols turned over on their heads at the birth of ʿĪsā and the devils became terrified and went to Iblīs, and they told him a [great] event had occured; so he [Iblīs] flew to the place of ʿĪsā's birth and saw angels circling round it, and he knew this was the site of the event. And the angels would not let him approach ʿĪsā. So, he [Iblīs] returned to his associates and informed them about that, and he said: "No woman gave birth except that I was present and it is my desire that more will be misguided [as a result of my presence] than those who are rightly guided."' *Tārīkh*, I, 312.

232 Qurṭubī, *Jāmiʿ*, IV, 68. Also see Qur'ān 3:36 '. . . I crave Thy protection for her and her offspring from Satan the outcast.'

233 *Jalālayn*, I, 113.

234 Zamakhsharī, *Kashshāf*, I, 142. Ṭabarī, *Jāmiʿ*, III, 239-40 and Thaʿlabī, *Qiṣaṣ*, 208 (on the authority of Qatāda). Rāzī criticises this ḥadīth saying that he personally does not think that God would give this privilege to Mary and Jesus without giving it to all other prophets: see *Mafātīḥ*, II, 459.

235 Muslim, *Ṣaḥīḥ*, XVI, 162, Kitāb ṣifa al-qiyāma wa al-janna wa al-nār, Bāb akthar al-aʿmal wa al-ijtihād fī al-ʿibāda.

236 Ibid., XV, 198, Kitāb al-faḍā'il; and Nawawī defines '*tharīd*' as a dish preferred by the Prophet (ﷺ) above all others, consisting of thin Arab bread soaked in a vegetable or meat stew. *Ṣaḥīḥ al-Bukhārī* in Ibn Ḥajar, *Fatḥ*, VI,

446, Kitāb al-Anbiyā, Bāb 32 (no. 3411) and 472-73, Bāb 47 (no. 3433): Also see 447, according to Ibn Ḥajar, 'It is said that the wife of the Pharaoh, Āsiya, was Mūsā's aunt, and it is said that she was an Amalekite [of the people of Canaan], and it is said that she was the paternal cousin of Pharaoh'; Qurṭubī, *Jāmiᶜ*, IV, 83; Ibn Kathīr, *Qiṣaṣ*, II, 379; Walī Allāh, *Ta'wīl*, 52–53.

237 Nawawī in *Ṣaḥīḥ Muslim*, XV, 198.

238 Ibn Kathīr, *Qiṣaṣ*, II, 380. Also, Ibn Kathīr, *Tafsīr*, IV, 394: He includes a different version from the previously mentioned one, which includes Khadīja as well as Mary and Āsiya.

239 Rosenthal, *Muslim Scholar*, 13: 'The formula: *Ṣallā Allāhu ᶜalayhi wa sallama*, is reserved for prophets and angels, and used immediately after they have been mentioned. According to custom and religious law, this formula is restricted to prophets and angels.'

240 The reference is to the *ᶜulamā'* of the medieval Spanish Muslims.

241 Qurṭubī's clarification seems to be based on the following *āya*: 'Whoso obeyeth God and the messenger, they are with those unto whom God hath shown favour, of the prophets and the saints and the martyrs and the righteous. The best of company are they!' (4:68).

242 Qurṭubī, *Jāmiᶜ*, IV, 83.

243 Ibid., IV, 82; 86; XI, 338.

244 Ibid., XI, 90.

245 see Qur'ān 19:16–21.

246 Qurṭubī, *Jāmiᶜ*, VI, 251.

247 Ibn Ḥajar, *Fatḥ*, VI, 447.

248 Ibid., 470.

249 Ibid., 470; 447–48. Ibn Ḥajar further asserts that it has been transmitted on the authority of al-Ashᶜarī that there have been some prophets amongst women.

250 Ibn Ḥazm, *Fiṣal*, V, 12.

251 Ibid., 12–13.

252 Ibid., 13.

253 Also see Qur'ān 20:38–40.

254 See the ḥadīth cited above in this chapter: 'Among men, there are many who have been perfect . . .'

255 Ibn Ḥazm, *Fiṣal*, 14, and 12–14 for all previous references to Ibn Ḥazm's discussion of Mary as prophetess.

256 Rāzī, *Tafsīr*, II, 461.

257 Ibid., 457. Also see Ibn Ḥazm's logical discussion of these points above.

258 Rāzī, *Tafsīr*, II, 467.

259 Ibid., 468.

260 *awliyā'* (plural of *walī*): friends of God; popularly, 'saints.'

261 al-Isfarā'inī was one of Ibn Fūrak's teachers of Ashʿarite theology: see *Encycl. of Islam* (new ed.) III, 766. See footnote 263 below for Ibn Fūrak.

262 Qushayrī, *Risāla*, II, 660.

263 Qushayrī studied with Abū Bakr Muḥammad ibn al-Ḥasan ibn Fūrak al-Anṣārī al-Iṣbahānī (c.941/330–1015/406), an Ashʿarite theologian and traditionist. His writings include discussions of whether a saint may know he is a saint and the sinlessness of prophets, and other theological topics: see Watt's article in *Encycl. of Islam* (new ed.), III, 766-67.

264 Qushayrī, *Risāla*, 661.

265 Qushayrī, *Risāla*, II, 662. However, Qushayrī's condition does not apply to Mary with respect to her miraculous provisions or her encounter with Gabriel at the time of the annunciation or the miracle of her conception of Jesus, none of which were provided as a result of her desire and request (*duʿā'*) for them.

266 al-Qushayri, *Risāla*, II, 664.

267 Ibid.

268 Ibid., 667. Also see Baljon, 'Prophetology', 73 for his reference to Shāh Walī Allāh's differentiation between prophets, *ḥakīms* and *walīs*: 'Unlike the prophets and *ḥakīms*, the *walīs* cannot give effective guidance to the community as a whole, because they are not in possession of the theoretical as well as the practical knowledge, a combination which is requisite to leadership.'

269 Qushayrī, *Risāla*, II, 667.

270 Qushayrī, *Laṭā'if*, I, 249; 254.

271 Shāh Walī Allāh, *Ta'wīl*, 5, 52-53. Baljon, 'Prophetology', 74; also see 69: Baljon says that Ibn ʿArabī uses *al-Wilāyah* (the state of being a saint) as the basis for all spiritual ranks, whereas that of prophet is important to Shāh Walī Allāh.

272 Usually described as *al-ʿaql al-faʿʿāl*.

273 Based on Baljon's synthesis of *al-Khayr al-Kathīr*, *khizāna*, 4,7: see Baljon, 'Prophetology', 74. *Sirr*: secret; secret heart, inner consciousness;

seat of the light of Unity (*tawḥīd*): see Zirr and Durkee, *Shādhdhuliyyah*, I, xxii for further references to this complex subject.

274 Shāh Walī Allāh, *Ta'wīl*, 5.

275 Baljon, 'Prophetology', 74.

276 Shāh Walī Allāh, *Ta'wīl*, 52-53.

277 Ibid., 53-56. For reference to John, see Qur'ān (3:38-40) and (19:15).

278 Ghurāb, *Tafsīr Ibn ʿArabī*, III, 39, 46.

279 Ibid., 39.

280 Ghurāb, *Tafsīr Ibn ʿArabī*, III, 45.

281 *al-ḥaqq*: 'The Real can be viewed in respect of the Essence or in respect of the name *Allāh*. The terms Essence and Divinity are applied to the same Reality, but from different points of view.' Chittick, *Sufi Path*, 49.

282 Zirr and Durkee, *Shādhdhuliyyah*, I, xii: '*jadhb* = attraction by Allah of whom He chooses.' Also see ad-Darqāwī, *Sufi Master*, Burckhardt, trans. & notes, 4; cf. note 1: 'One who is attracted by the divine attraction, the spiritual person whose Spirit is continuously absent from the plane of the sense and reason.'

283 '*Murāqaba* is the constant state of [spiritual] vigilance such that there is not a moment in which the slave [of Allah] forsakes it,' Ibn ʿArabī, *Futūḥāt*, II, 209 (Bāb 126 fī maʿrifat maqām al-murāqaba). Just prior to this definition, Ibn ʿArabī describes three aspects of the station of *murāqaba*, the last of which applies to its use in the above text of Rūzbihān: 'And the third *murāqaba* is that one sits in observation of his "heart" [organ of the *rūḥ*/spirit] and his *nafs* [passional soul/ego]—the outer and the inward—in order to see the traces/signs of his Lord in them, then he acts, taking into account what he sees of the traces/signs of the Lord.' (Ibid.) Also see *Futūḥāt*, I, 176 (Bāb 22, Manzil al-barakāt) for Ibn ʿArabī's explanation of *murāqaba* in the context of the state achieved by the seeker of *barakāt al-ziyāda*. Also see Zirr and Durkee, *Shādhdhuliyyah*, I, 26 who quote Ibn Ṣabbāgh, *Durrat al-asrār* that *murāqaba* is: 'sitting upon the carpet of watchfulness and rendering sincere your inner life until there remains nothing that He has forbidden.' See Chittick, *Sufi Path*, 348 for his definition of *murāqaba*. See Ghurāb, *Tafsīr Ibn ʿArabī*, III, 43, for Ibn ʿArabī's perception of Mary's state of vigilance and the nature of Gabriel.

284 Zirr and Durkee, *Shādhdhuliyyah*, I, 71 for Shaykh Muḥammad al-Jamāl ar-Rifā'ī ash-Shādhdhulī's description of *jabarūt*: 'And the stations

of the Way lead to the reservoir of *al-jabarūt* (the World of Sovereignty or the Presence of the Secrets) from whence the brilliant lights of his [Muḥammad's] Secret pour out in abundance . . . The World of Sovereignty (*al-jabarūt*) is like the sea whose shores are the gardens which are watered by the reservoirs. The lights of the Prophet are the water used to irrigate those gardens and it is constantly flowing in great effusion.' Also see 23 for the diagram in which *jabarūt*, is just above *al-malakūt*.

285 Ibn ʿArabī, *Futūḥāt*, II, 176 (Bāb 91 fī maʿrifat al-waraʿ wa asrārihi), in which he explains that the effects of the union of the property of Divine Attributes with the station of the slave of God manifests itself in the slave's world of *mulk*, his world of *jabarūt* and/or his world of *malakūt*. Cf. note 287 below for differences in translation of *mulk* and *malakūt*.

286 In addition to the usual geographical meaning of the word 'East', the East in Islamic mysticism represents a metaphysical orientation which is generally understood to be the point(s) of orientation of the spirit which open(s) to spiritual ascent from one world to the next higher one, in this case the *malakūt* to the *jabarūt*. Ibn ʿArabī, *Futūḥāt*, I, 107 (Bāb 5 fī maʿrifat asrār Bismillāh al-Raḥmān al-Raḥīm—Waṣl qawlihi al-Raḥmān), defines *al-mashriq* as: 'The orientation existing in the line (between the Known and the Unknown) [. . .] And the manifestation (of light) which results from the acceptance, by Allah's Will, to go wherever one is carried by His Will (*al-ẓāhir al-murakkab*); see the poem on the same page describing '*al-ẓāhir*' as 'light.' Also see *Futūḥāt*, I, 203-6 (Bāb 31 fī maʿrifat uṣūl al-rukkāb) in which Khiḍr is the primary example of the *rukkāb*.

287 Chittick, *Sufi Path*, 282 translates '*mulk*' as 'the kingdom' and '*malakūt*' as 'the domain'; this book; however, will follow Winter's translation of these terms: see al-Ghazālī, *Remembrance of Death* (Winter trans. & notes), xxi, "ʿ*ālam al-malakūt*: the world of the Attributes, in contrast to ʿ*ālam al-mulk*: the material world'; and 139, cf (B): 'The Kingdom, the highest of the three planes of existence found in al-Ghazālī's cosmology'; and 149: 'Upon his death, man passes from the Terrestrial and Visible Realm (ʿ*ālam al-mulk wa'l-shahāda*) to the Realm of the Unseen and the Kingdom (ʿ*ālam al-ghayb wa'l-malakūt*).' On p. 150, al-Ghazālī explains that if the veil is removed from the 'heart's eye', man can behold the Kingdom—i.e., such as the prophets, the *awliyā'* and in dreams for other righteous persons.

288 Zirr and Durkee, *Shādhdhuliyyah*, I, xi: '*al-himmah* = ardent effort; extreme longing for Allah, spiritual will.'

289 Zirr and Durkee, *Shādhdhuliyyah*, I, 23; diagram of the realms of existence, illustrating that '*dhāt*' is the Ultimate Essence which man can perceive, as man is incapable of perceiving the Unknowable, Ultimate Essence; and viii: '*adh-dhāt* = essence, ipseity; that which displays *ṣifāt* (attributes) but which is beyond the hypostases, the ground, the universal medium.' Also see Burckhardt's note in Darqāwī, *Letters*, 20: '*Adh-dhāt* is the Essence in the absolute meaning of the word [as far as man can perceive], the ultimate reality to which all qualities relate.'

290 *al-azal*: 'beginninglessness': see Chittick, *Sufi Path*, 62, 64, 100. see Ibn ʿArabī, *Futūḥāt*, I, 160 (Bāb 16 fi maʿrifat al-manzil as-salafiyya wa al-ʿulūm al-kawniyya, Faṣl: wa ammā maʿrifat al-ḥaqq min hādhā al-manzil): 'And to us, there is no difference of opinion about the fact that the Essence cannot be known, rather non-anthropomorphic Attributes are emanated from It—descriptions [at the level] of the temporal world [al-*ḥadath*], among which is Eternity [*al-qidam*] and Beginninglessness [*al-azal*], which frees Its existence of [the characteristic of limitation]'; and in I, 188 of Bāb 26, Ibn ʿArabī provides knowledge of 'the secret' of *al-azal*. For Chittick's translation of the above passage (i.e., *Futūḥāt*, I, 160), see *Sufi Path*, 62.

291 For *qidam*, see previous footnote. For '*mushāhada*,' see Chittick, *Sufi Path*, 225: 'Another important synonym for unveiling is 'witnessing' [*shuhūd, mushāhada*]. This term has a wider sense than unveiling since it is commonly used for sight as well as insight,' and see 225-28 for a clear presentation and discussion of the term and of Ibn ʿArabī's texts on its technical meaning.

292 *al-kubrā*: i.e., the word which outranks all others.

293 'Of' in the sense of belonging to; i.e., that Allah is the sole Master of all His creations.

294 Chittick, *Sufi Path*, 37: 'Ibn al-ʿArabī and others employ the word 'reality' (*ḥaqiqā*) in a number of senses [. . .] The Shaykh [Ibn ʿArabī] often employs it more or less synonymously with name. A reality is the Divine Essence considered in respect of a particular relationship which It assumes with the creatures. This relationship may be specified by a revealed name, in which case the name demonstrates the reality. Strictly speaking, the reality is then the name itself, while the revealed name is the "name of the name".'

295 Rūzbihān al-Baqlī, *ʿArā'is*, II, 7. see Smith and Haddad, 'The Virgin', 183-84 for McCarthy's quite beautiful translation of this text,

which maintains the spirit of the original. Also see ʿAbd el-Jalīl, *Marie et l'Islam*, 80 for a literal translation into French of this text, a translation devoid of the intended mystical meanings.

296 See fuller definition of *al-fiṭra* in footnote 229.

297 Badawī, *Batūl*, 27–28.

298 The Qur'ān states that Allah has sent an apostle to every community (*umma*) (10:47; 16:36; 23:44; 40:45). Messengers cited by name in the Qur'ān are: Nūḥ (71:1), Lūṭ (7:80). Ismāʿīl (19:55), Mūsā (2:87), Shuʿayb (7:85), Ḥūd (11:50), Ṣāliḥ (7:73), Jesus (3:49), and Muḥammad (48:28-29). Abraham (87:19), Moses (87:19), Jesus (19:30), and Muḥammad (48-29) are cited as having been given a Book. Although there is evidence of the Books of Moses, Jesus, and Muḥammad, as well as their respective spiritual communities, the Book of Abraham is no longer extant. For those scholars who do not differentiate between messenger (*rasūl*) and prophet (*nabī*), the number listed would be considerably greater. See *Shorter Encycl. of Islam*, 470.

299 Naṣr, *Ideals*, 43-44. Also see Barr, "ʿĪsā', XXXIII,4 (1989), 257, note.

300 For this reason, in controversial exegeses, the Prophet Muḥammad has been described as the counterpart of Mary (not Jesus), both being the vehicle of the Word: see Ibn ʿArabī, *Futūḥāt*, I, 111, Bab 5 fi maʿrifat asrār Bismillāh al-Raḥmān al-Raḥīm wa al-Fātiḥa min jāmiʿat al-wujūh, Faṣl fi asrār Umm al-Qur'ān min ṭarīq khāṣṣ. Also, Hitti, *Islam and the West*, 13.

301 If one is addressing the traditional Sunni perspective on Mary, the Rev. Kerr's assessment that it is an overstatement to say that 'Most Muslim commentators accept Mary as a prophet' seems valid (See Kerr, 'Mary', 17). However, based on the classical Sunni sources examined, I have not found evidence for McAuliffe's conclusion that Mary is 'backstaged' by Fāṭima ('Chosen of all women', 28) nor for her conclusion that the 'majority of Sunnis' would confirm that 'Fāṭīma's status as the first female in Islam is unchallenged' (28). Her strongest bases for this conclusion appear to be non-Sunni sources (23; 26–27). Also see ʿAbd-el-Jalīl, *Marie et l'Islam*, 76-77, for his general assessment that Mary is superior to Fāṭima in Islam.

302 *dīwān*: a collection of poetry.

303 Littmann, 'Islamische-arabische Heiligenlieder', 110–35. Littmann states that he found the *dīwān* in a small publication entitled *Maḥāsin al-durar*

fī dīwān al-dabb wa'l-ḥajar, Cairo: al-Maktaba al-Mulūkiyya, n.d., and he had it recited in Egyptian colloquial to the rhythm of the tamborine by Maḥmūd Ṣidqī, his assistant/informant (Gewährsmann). He also notes that the rhyming scheme of this *dīwān* (a, a, a, b) differs from the usual (a, a, b, a) see 101–2.

304 See Qur'ān 19:16–32 for the section about Mary, Pickthall trans., *Glorious Koran,* 395: 'Surah Maryam is a Makkan surah, except for ayats 57 and 71, which were revealed in Al-Madinah.'

305 See Umm Salama's account in Ibn Hisham, *Sīra,* I, 289-90; Ibn Kathīr's presentation (*Sīra,* II, 17-21, and 20), which culminates with Umm Salama's account only; also Aḥmad ibn Ḥanbal, *Musnad,* I, 201–3; V, 290-92, for Umm Salama's account only; also Bayhaqī, *Dalā'il,* II, 70-73 (a well-organised presentation, which clearly separates the accounts by different narrators). Maqdisī, *Bad',* IV, 152 (a brief summary, basically containing the same elements found in Umm Salama's account, but lacking sources.)

306 The term 'Morisco' was used to describe the secret Muslims who remained in Spain after the fall of Granada in 1492, having been nominally baptised: see *Diccionario,* 694; Lomax, *Reconquest,* 172. The majority of Moriscos continued to adhere to the *farḍ* (obligatory) practices in Islam, the legal tenets (Mālikī law for most), and the voluntary acts; see Lenker, 'Riḥla', 70; Longás y Bartibás, *Vida,* XVIV; *Encycl. of Islam* (new ed.), I, 497; García-Arenal, *Los Moriscos,* 89–95; De Bunes, *Los Moriscos,* 76; Gayangos, 'Language and Literature,' 78. The language of many Morisco texts is Aljamía (from Ar. '*al-ʿajamiyya*'): see *Diccionario,* 51. Aljamía generally represents the Romance language written in Maghribī Arabic characters, while preserving technical Islamic expressions through the use of a facsimile of the Arabic phrase. For the other definitions, see Epalza, 'Manuscritto', 35 and Gayangos, 'Language and Literature', 92.

307 Chejne's assessment that the Moriscos 'devoted more space' to the Islamic conception of Christ 'owing to the Christian environment in which they lived and to the need to give ample proof of the truth of Islam vis-à-vis Christianity' (*Islam and the West,* 108) appears to be equally applicable to Maryam.

308 *al-ḥajjī*: the pilgrim.

309 *Encycl. of Islam* (new ed.), I, 405.

310 Prior to the advent of aeroplanes, participation in the pilgrimage to Makka involved a long, arduous journey by land, and by sea,

depending on the country of origin of the pilgrim. The journey could take a year or more, traversing those countries which were along the established routes. Crossing Egypt formed part of one of the main pilgrimage routes.

311 This is my literal translation of the meaning and unfortunately does not conserve the beauty of the original.

312 'Figuera' = fig tree. Pano y Ruata, *Las Coplas del Peregrino de Puey Monçón*, 63. From the subsequent verses, it appears to be a miraculous tree.

313 Ibid., 63-64.

314 *Las Coplas*, 65-66.

315 Ar.: *al-khuṭba* = sermon.

316 Longás y Bartibás, *Vida*, 169.

317 Hegyi, *Cinco Leyendas*, 105-106: My translation of Hegyi's transliteration of the Aljamiado text follows. Also see Longás y Bartibás, *Vida*, 105-96 for his Spanish translation of this text.

318 See Harvey, 'Literary Culture'; and Narváez, 'El Mancebo,' 109-15. This sixteenth-century Aljamía manuscript, no. LXII, is found in the collection of Ribera and Asín, Instituto de Filología, Madrid.

319 See for example footnote 326 below. After transliterating this section of the manuscript, I adjusted my English translation to conform with that of Narváez' Spanish translation, with a few footnoted exceptions.

320 See Narváez, 'El Mancebo', 110, who cites this expression for its pointed depiction of Mary's virginity.

321 *Ṣaḥīḥ Muslim*, XVI, 210, Kitāb al-qadr, Bāb kull mawlūd ʿalā al-fiṭra, for the sound ḥadīth: 'There is no child born without the touch [prod] of Satan [. . .] except the son of Mary and his mother.'

322 Appears to be '*votiva*,' i.e., 'one who was offered by a vow'.

323 The corresponding term in Islamic mysticism is '*himma*.'

324 *vía* = Ar.: *ṭarīqa*.

325 '*Adoptiva*' according to Narváez, 'El Mancebo', 109. The reference may be to Zachariah's guardianship.

326 As a jewel is set in silver or gold—both the Spanish word '*engastonado*' (Old Sp. for '*engastado*') and its corresponding Arabic term '*murakkab*' have this meaning. For the underlying mystical meaning, see Ibn ʿArabī, *Futūḥāt*, I, 202.

327 In this context, '*hija*' appears to mean 'nun': see *Diccionario*, 545 (def. no. 3).

328 Narváez, 'El Mancebo', 109 does not translate this term, presumably part of El Mancebo's special religious vocabulary.

329 This is meant allegorically.

330 See Chittick, *Sufi Path*, 49; Zirr and Durkee, *Shādhdhuliyyah*, I, viii, 23, for the mystical meaning of this expression in Islam.

331 *Abdo* = Ar.: "ʿ*abīd*' (slaves of Allah). Narváez, 'El Mancebo', 109 renders '*abdo tomadox*' as one word '*abdutumados*' (dedicated, consecrated).

332 Narváez, 'El Mancebo', 109, translates '*nozimientos*' as '*daños*', perhaps from *nuez* (vomica: a poisonous fruit), i.e., something which is harmful.

333 *Asud* = Ar.: *al-sadd*: barrier. Narváez, 'El Mancebo', 110, in which she says that El Mancebo dedicated a chapter to this theme. He says that '*el-asuwd*', is a light of invisible darkness (*lámpara de tinieblas invisibles*), and the Qur'ānic commentators distinguish three types of '*el-asuwd*', one of which applies to Mary: Another '*asuwd*' [is] that of [Divine] Grace, which the sages appease by the means of the virtue inherent in certain '*aleas*' (verses, sūras) of the Qur'ān. Gabriel uses this '*asuwd*' to aid the just and the wise in their tribulations. Thus, it is a question of Divine favour that is obtained by means of virtue and that permits the intervention of Gabriel on the side of the believer. It is undoubtedly this '*asuwd*' of [Divine] Grace that Mary possesses.

334 Narváez, 'El Mancebo', 109 renders '*anpara*' as '*lámpara*' (light).

335 I.e., not to protect the eyes, but to protect the heart.

336 This may be compared to the text of Rūzbihān al-Baqlī, see ʿ*Arā'is*, II, 7; and Ibn ʿArabī, *Futūḥāt*, II, 209, Bāb 126 fī maʿrifat maqām al-murāqaba, the third definition, for a relevant understanding of *murāqaba* in Islamic mysticism.

337 See Qur'ān 5:47–51.

338 See Waddy, *Women*, 34, who especially cites the *miḥrāb* of the mosque of Santa Sophia in Istanbul.

339 The Juyūshī Mosque and tomb was built in 478/1085 by the *wazīr* Badr al-Jamālī to hold his sepulchre: see *Encycl. of Islam* (new ed.), II, 863.

340 *qibla*: the direction which Muslims face when performing the ritual prayers. The second *qibla* is the Kaʿba.

341 The first *qibla* was Jerusalem. Prior to approximately sixteen and a half months after the Hijra (emigration) to al-Madīna, the *qibla* for the Muslims was Jerusalem. Qur'ān 2:142–43; Yūsuf ʿAlī (trans.), *Holy Qur'ān*; and *Shorter Encycl. of Islam*, 260.

Notes to Appendix

1 Haykal, *Ḥayāt*, 118. Also, Grabar, *Islamic Art*, 80: 'When the Ka'bah was rebuilt in 605, it was done by a foreign carpenter with the help of a Coptic assistant.'

2 Parrinder, *Jesus*, 66 (via the *Encycl. of Islam* via Cresswell). Also, Cresswell, *Early Muslim Architecture*, 2, 97.

3 Azraqī, *Akhbār*. (Although in 1, 73 Azraqī makes a general statement that he uses Wahb ibn Munabbih as a transmitter.]

4 Ibrāhīm al-Khalīl (ﷺ): Abraham, the beloved friend of God.

5 Azraqī, *Akhbār*, 1, 165-66.

6 Ibid., 165, cf. (5).

7 *Ṣaḥīḥ al-Bukhārī* in Ibn Ḥajar, *Fatḥ*, VIII, 16: Kitāb al-Maghāzī, Bāb (48) (no. 4288); also VI, 387, Kitāb al-Anbiyā, Bāb (8) (nos. 3351-52) for further versions.

8 Ibid., VIII, 17.

9 Abū Dāwūd, *Sunan*, IV, 74; Kitāb al-Libās (Suwar) (no. 4156). Also Azraqī, *Akhbār*, 1, 166, cf. (5).

10 Wāqidī, Maghāzī, II, 834. There is another apparently corrupt account, which begins with 'Zuhrī *used to say*,' and states that the Prophet (ﷺ) saw a picture of Mary, 'and he placed his hand over it; then he said: Ḙrase all the pictures, except the picture of Abraham'.

11 Ibid.

12 Azraqī, *Akhbār*, 1, 165, cf. (5).

13 Ibid.

14 The above version is from Aḥmad ibn Ḥanbal, *Musnad*, 1, 104 (for 14 other versions, see vols. 1, 2, 4, and 6); *Ṣaḥīḥ al-Bukhārī* in Ibn Ḥajar, *Fatḥ*, X, 391-393; *Kitāb al-Libās*, see Bāb (94) for Jibril's refusal to enter . . .; Bāb (95) for 'Ā'isha and the cushion with pictures . . . ; Bāb (96) for a comparison of the creator of pictures with the usurer . . . ; *Ṣaḥīḥ Muslim*, XIV, 84, Kitāb al-Libās wa az-Zīna, Bāb Taḥrīm Sūra al-Ḥayawān; Abū Dāwūd, *Sunan*, IV, 42-43, Kitāb al-Libās (Suwar) (no. 4152); Nasā'ī, *Sunan*, VII, 185, Kitāb aṣ-Ṣayd and VIII, 212, Kitāb az-Zīna. Also see Grabar, *Islamic Art*, chap. 4, 'Islamic Attitudes toward the Arts.'

15 *Ṣaḥīḥ Muslim*, XIV, 91.

16 Ibid., 84.

17 *Ṣaḥīḥ al-Bukhārī* in Ibn Ḥajar, *Fatḥ*, VII, 187-88. Kitāb Manāqib al-Ansār, Bāb (37) (no. 3873). See 189, Ibn Ḥajar says this (conversation) occurred after the second emigration to Abyssinia. (This abhorrence of a place of worship containing pictures and other images demonstrated by the Prophet was equally strong in the caliphs, see al-Suyūṭī, *Faḍā'il*, I, 239, for ʿUmar's reaction to praying in the Church of Mary.)

18 *Ṣaḥīḥ Muslim*, XIV, 92-93, Kitāb al-Libās wa az-Zīna, Bāb Taḥrīm Taṣwīr Ṣūrat al-Ḥayawān.

19 Azraqī, *Akhbār*, I, 165, cf. (5) for Mulḥas' statement.

20 The *qāḍī* is a judge whose decisions are based on Islamic law (*Sharīʿa*).

21 See *Shorter Encycl. of Islam*, 554, for mention of those scholars who assert that all images are forbidden in Islam and for the justification of their position.

Bibliography

The Glorious Koran (Arabic & English text). Translated by Marmaduke Pickthall. London: George Allen and Unwin, 1969.

The Holy Qur'an (Arabic and English text). Translated by ʿAbdullah Yūsuf ʿAlī. U.S.A: McGregor and Werner Inc., 1946.

The Koran. Translated by N.J. Dawood. Harmondsworth: Penguin, 1968.

The Koran. Translated by George Sale. London: Frederick Warne and Co. Ltd., n.d.

The Koran Interpreted. Translated by Arthur J. Arberry. London: Oxford University Press, 1964.

The Message of the Qur'an (Arabic and English text). Translated by Muḥammad Asad. Gibraltar: Dār al-Andalus, 1980.

The King James Bible (Authorised Version). New York: Delair Publishing Co., Inc.,1982.

PRIMARY SOURCES

Abū Dāwūd al-Sijistānī, Sulaymān ibn al-Ashʿath (d. 275 AH) *Al-Sunan.* Beirut: Dār al-Fikr, n.d.

al-Azraqī, Abu'l-Walīd Muḥammad ibn ʿAbdullāh (ninth century CE), ed. Rushdī al-Ṣāliḥ Mulḥas. *Akhbār Makka.* Beirut: Dār al-Andalus, 1969.

al-Bayḍāwī, ʿAbdullāh ibn ʿUmar. *Anwār al-Tanzīl wa Asrār al-Ta'wīl.* In margin of Jalāl al-Dīn ʿAbd al-Raḥmān al-Suyūṭī and Jalāl al-Dīn Muḥammad al-Maḥallī. *Tafsīr al-Jalālayn.* Cairo: al-Maṭbaʿat al-Maymaniyya, 1902.

al-Bayhaqī, Abū Bakr Aḥmad ibn al-Ḥusayn (d. 458 AH). *Dalā'il al-Nubuwwa*. Ed. ʿAbd al-Raḥmān Muḥammad ʿUthmān. Cairo: Dār al-Fikr, 1983/1403.

al-Bukhārī, Muḥammad ibn Ismāʿīl (810/194-870/256). *al-Jāmiʿ al-Ṣaḥīḥ* (see Ibn Ḥajar).

al-Dhahabī, Shams al-Dīn Muḥammad ibn Aḥmad. *Siyar Aʿlām al-Nubalā'*. Cairo: Dār al-Maʿārif, 1957.

———. *Tārīkh al-Islām wa-Ṭabaqāt al-Mashāhīr wa'l-Aʿlām*. Cairo: Dār al-Kutub al-Miṣrīya, 1985.

al-Ghazālī, Abū Ḥamid Muḥammad ibn Muḥammad (d. 505 AH). *Iḥyā ʿUlūm al-Dīn* (and in the footnotes: al-Imām al-ʿIrāqī (d. 806 AH), *al-Mughnī ʿan Ḥaml al-Asfār fī'l-Asfār fī Takhrīj mā fī'l-Iḥyā' min al-Akhbār)*. Cairo: Dār al-Rayān li'l-Turāth, 1987/1407.

al-Ghurāb, Maḥmūd Maḥmūd (ed). *Raḥmat min al-Raḥmān fī Tafsīr wa-Ishārāt al-Qur'ān: Min Kalām al-Shaykh al-Akbar Muḥyī al-Dīn ibn al-ʿArabī*. Damascus: Maṭbaʿat Naḍr, 1989/1410.

(Ḥājjī Khalīfa), Muṣṭafā ibn ʿAbdullāh al-Qustanṭīnī al-Rūmī al-Ḥanafī (d. 1067 AH). *Kashf al-Ẓunūn ʿan Asāmī al-Kutub wa'l-Funūn*. Beirut: Dār al-Fikr, 1982/1402.

al-Ḥallāj al-Bayḍāwī al-Baghdādī, al-Ḥusayn ibn Manṣūr. (With commentary by Rūzbihān al-Baqlī) (ed. Louis Massignon). Paris: Librairie Paul Geuthner, 1913.

Ibn ʿAbd Rabbihi al-Andalusī (d. 940/328). *Al-ʿIqd al-Farīd*. Cairo: Maṭbaʿat al-Istiqāma, 1953/1372.

———. *Ṭabā'iʿ al-Insān wa'l-Ḥayawān*. Beirut: Dār Ṣādir, 1953.

Ibn (al-) ʿArabī, Muḥyī al-Dīn (d. 638 AH). *Al-Futūḥāt al-Makkiyya*. Beirut: Dār Ṣādir, n.d. (4 vols.)

———. (See: al-Ghurāb).

Ibn ʿAsākir, al-Imām Abū al-Qāsim ʿAlī ibn al-Ḥasan (d. 1175/571), *Tahdhīb Tārīkh Dimāshq al-Kabīr*. Beirut: Dār al-Masīra. [Originally published 1331].

Ibn al-Athīr, Muḥammad ibn ʿAbd al-Karīm ibn ʿAbd al-Waḥīd al-Shaybānī. *Al-Kāmil fī'l-Tārīkh*. Beirut: Dār Ṣādir, 1965.

(Ibn Baṭṭūṭa) Muḥammad ibn ʿAbdullāh (b.1304/703). *Tuḥfat al-Nuẓẓār bi-Gharā'ib al-Amṣār wa ʿAjā'ib al-Asfār*. Egypt: Dār al-Kitāb al-Miṣrī, n.d.

Ibn Ḥajar al-ʿAsqalānī, Shihāb al-Dīn Abū al-Faḍl Aḥmad ibn ʿAlī. (d. 853 AH) *Fatḥ al-Bārī* (with the complete text of *Ṣaḥīḥ al-Bukhārī*). al-Maktabat al-Salafiyya, n.d.

———. *Lisān al-Mīzān*. Beirut: Mu'assasat al-ʿĀlamī li'l-Maṭbūʿāt, 1971/1390 (2d print.).

Ibn Ḥanbal, al-Imām Aḥmad. *al-Musnad*. Beirut: Dār al-Fikr, n.d.

Ibn Ḥazm al-Andalusī, ʿAlī ibn Aḥmad (d. 456 AH). *Al-Fiṣal fī al-milal wa'l-Ahwā' wa'l-Niḥal*. (and in the margin) al-Shahrastānī (d. 548 AH), *al-Milal wa'l-Niḥal*. Cairo: Maṭbaʿat Muḥammad ʿAlī Ṣabīḥ and sons, 1928.

Ibn Hishām, Abū Muḥammad ʿAbd al-Mālik. *al-Sīrat al-Nabawiyya*. Beirut: Dār al-Jīl, 1975.

Ibn Ḥusām al-Dīn al-Hindī, ʿAlā' al-Dīn ʿAlī al-Muttaqī (957 AH). *Kanz al-ʿUmmāl fī Sunan al-Aqwāl*. Beirut: Mu'assasat al-Risāla, 1979/1399.

Ibn al-Jawzī, Jamāl al-Dīn Abū al-Farāj ʿAbd al-Raḥmān. *Faḍā'il al-Quds*. Beirut: Dār al-Āfāq al-Jadīda, 1980/1400.

Ibn Kathīr al-Qurashī al-Dimashqī, al-Imām ʿImād al-Dīn Abū al-Fidā' Ismāʿīl (d. 747 AH). *Tafsīr al-Qur'ān al-ʿAẓīm*. Cairo: Dār Iḥyā' al-Kutub al-ʿArabiyya, n.d.

———. *Qiṣaṣ al-Anbiyā'*. Cairo: Dār al-Kutub, 1968/1388.

———. *al-Sīrat al-Nabawiyya*. Cairo: Maṭbaʿat ʿĪsā al-Bābī al-Ḥalabī wa-Shurakāhu, 1966/1386.

Ibn Manẓūr al-Ifrīqī al-Miṣrī, Abū Faḍl Jamāl al-Dīn Muḥammad ibn Makram. *Lisān al-ʿArab*. Beirut: Dār Ṣādir. n.d.

Ibn Qayyim al-Jawziyya, al-Imām Shams al-Dīn Abū ʿAbdullāh. *al-Tafsīr al-Qayyim*. Beirut: Lajnat al-Turāth al-ʿArabī, n.d.

———. *Hidāyat al-Ḥayārā fī Ajwibat al-Yuhūd wa'l-Naṣārā*. Cairo: Maktabat al-Qīma, 1978/1399.

Ibn Qutayba, Abū Muḥammad ʿAbdullāh ibn Muslim. *Ta'wīl Mushkil al-Qur'an*, ed. Aḥmad Saqr. Cairo: Dār Iḥyā' al-Kutub al-ʿArabiyya, 1954.

———. *Al-Maʿārif*. Cairo: Dār al-Maʿārif, 1969.

Ibn al-Ṣabbāgh al-Ḥumayrī. *Durrat al-Asrār*. Cairo: Maṭbaʿat al-Saʿāda, 1988/1408.

Ibn Saʿd (Kātib al-Wāqidī), Muḥammad (d. c. 230 AH). *Al-Ṭabaqāt al-Kubrā*. Beirut: Dār al-Kutub al-ʿIlmiyya, 1983/1403.

Ibn Taymiyya, Aḥmad ibn ʿAbd al-Ḥalīm. *al-Jawāb al-Ṣaḥīḥ liman Baddala Dīn al-Masīḥ*. Maṭbaʿat al-Nabl, 1905.

al-Khāzin al-Baghdādī al-Ṣūfī, ʿAlā' al-Dīn ʿAlī ibn Muḥammad. *Tafsīr al-Khāzin* (and in the margin:) *Tafsīr al-Nasafī*. Cairo: Maṭbaʿat al-Taqaddum, 1912.

al-Maqdisī, al-Muṭahhar ibn Ṭāhir. *Kitāb al-Bad' wa'l-Tārīkh*, ed. C. Huart. Paris: Leroux, 1903.

al-Maqrīzī, Taqī al-Dīn Aḥmad ibn ʿAlī ibn ʿAbd al-Qādir. *Kitāb al-Mawāʿiẓ wa'l-ʿIʿtibār fī Dhikr al-Khiṭaṭ wa'l-Athār.*, ed. Gaston Wiet. Cairo: French Archeological Institute, 1923.

al-Marghinānī, Burhān al-Dīn ʿAlī ibn Abū Bakr. *Kitāb al-Hidāya*. Cairo: Maṭbaʿat al-Khayriyya, 1326 AH.

Mujāhid ibn Jabr al-Tābʿī al-Makkī al-Makhzūmī. *Tafsīr Mujāhid*. Beirut: al-Manshūrat al-ʿIlmiyya, 1921/1469.

Muqātil ibn Sulaymān al-Balkhī. *Tafsīr Muqātil ibn Sulaymān*. Cairo: Mu'assasat al-Ḥalabī wa Shurakāhu, 1969.

Muslim ibn al-Ḥajjāj, al-Imām Abu'l-Ḥasan. *Ṣaḥīḥ Muslim (bi-sharḥ al-Nawawī)*. Cairo: al-Maṭbaʿat al-Miṣriyya, 1924.

al-Nasafī, ʿAbdullāh Aḥmad ibn Maḥmūd (d. 1310). *Tafsīr Madārik al-Tanzīl wa-Ḥaqā'iq al-Ta'wil*. Cairo: Maktabat wa Maṭbaʿat Muḥammad ʿAlī Ṣabīḥ wa Awlādihi, 1948.

al-Nasā'ī, al-Imām Abū ʿAbd al-Raḥmān Aḥmad ibn Shuʿayb. *Sunan (bi-sharḥ Jalāl al-Dīn al-Suyūṭī)*. Beirut: Dār al-Kitāb al-ʿArabī, n.d.

al-Nawawī (see Muslim).

Qurṭubī, Abū ʿAbdullāh Muḥammad ibn Aḥmad al-Anṣārī (d. 671 AH). *Al-Jāmiʿ li-Aḥkām al-Qur'ān*. Cairo: Dār al-Kātib al-ʿArabī li'l-Ṭabʿat wa'l-Nashr ʿan Ṭibāʿat Dār al-Kutub al-Miṣriyya, 1967/1387 (3d print.).

al-Qushayrī, Abu'l-Qāsim ʿAbd al-Karīm ibn Hawāzin (d. 365 AH) *Laṭā'if al-Ishārāt*. Cairo: Dār al-Kātib al-ʿArabī, n.d.

———. *al-Risālat al-Qushayriyya,* ed. ʿAbd al-Ḥalīm Maḥmūd and Maḥmūd ibn al-Sharīf. Cairo: Dār al-Kutub, n.d.

al-Rāzī, Fakhr al-Dīn Muḥammad ibn ʿUmar (d. c. 1210). *Mafātīḥ al-Ghayb: al-Tafsīr al-Kabīr* (and in the margin:) *Tafsīr al-ʿAllāmat Abu'l-Suʿūd.* Cairo: Maṭbaʿat al-Amīrat al-Sharqiyya, 1889/1308.

Rūzbihān al-Baqlī, Ibn Abī Naṣr. *ʿArā'is al-Bayān* (and in the margin:) Muḥyī al-Dīn ibn (al-) ʿArabī (attr.), *Tafsīr ʿAlāmihi* (from the Indian lithograph). Lucknow, 1301.

———. (see al-Ḥallāj).

al-Sakhāwī, Shams al-Dīn Muḥammad ibn ʿAbd al-Raḥmān (d. 902 AH) *Al-Iʿlān bi'l-Tawbīkh liman Dhamma al-Tārīkh.* Damascus: al-Qudsī, 1349 AH.

Shabistarī, Mahmoud. *Rosenflor des Geheimnisses (Gulshan-i Rāz)* (Persian and German texts). Tr. Hammer-Purgstall. Leipzig, 1838.

Ṣiddīq Khān, Muḥammad Ḥasan. *Ḥusn al-uswat bimā Thabat min Allāh wa Rasūlihi fi'l-Niswa.* Beirut: Mu'assasat al-Risāla, 1976.

al-Suyūtī, Muḥammad ibn Shihāb al-Dīn. *Itḥāf al-Akhiṣṣa bi Faḍā'il al-Masjid al-Aqṣā,* ed. Aḥmad Ramaḍān Aḥmad. Cairo: Maṭābiʿ al-Ḥay'at al-Miṣriyyat al-ʿĀmma li'l-Kitāb, 1982–84.

Ṭabarī, Abū Jaʿfar Muḥammad ibn Jarīr. *Jāmiʿ al-Bayān ʿan Ta'wīl Āī al-Qur'ān.* Cairo: Muṣṭafā al-Bābī al-Hālabī, 1968/1388 (3d print.).

———. *Tārīkh al-Rusul wa'l-Mulūk.* Cairo: Dār al-Maʿārif, 1960.

al-Thaʿlabī, Ibn Isḥāq Aḥmad ibn Muḥammad Ibrāhīm. *Qiṣaṣ al-Anbiyā.* (and in the margin:) al-Yāfiʿī, *Kitāb Rawḍ al-Rayāḥīn.* Dār al-Zahrā', n.d.

al-Thawrī al-Kūfī, Abū ʿAbdullāh Sufyān ibn Saʿīd ibn Masrūq. *Tafsīr al-Qur'ān al-Karīm.* (Pub. unknown), 1965.

(al-Wāqidī), Muḥammad ibn Wāqid (d. 208 AH), ed. J. Marsden Jones, *Kitāb al-Maghāzī li'l-Wāqidī.* London: Oxford University Press, 1966.

al-Wāsiṭī, Muḥammad ibn Aḥmad. *Faḍā'il al-Bayt al-Maqdis,* ed., Isaac Hasson. Hebrew University Press, 1979.

Yāqūt ibn ʿAbdullāh al-Ḥamawī, Shihāb al-Dīn Abū ʿAbdullāh. *Muʿjam al-Buldān.* Beirut: Dār Ṣādir, 1984/1404.

al-Zabīdi, Muḥammad ibn Muḥammad al-Ḥusaynī. *Tāj al-ʿArūs*. Kuwait: Maṭbaʿat al-Kuwayt, 1965/1385.

al-Zamakhsharī, Maḥmud ibn ʿUmar. *Al-Kashshāf ʿan Ḥaqā'iq Ghawāmiḍ al-Tanzīl wa ʿUyūn al-Aqāwīl fī Wujūh al-Ta'wīl*. Cairo: al-Maṭbaʿat al-Bahiyyat al-Miṣriyya, 1924-25/1343-44.

SECONDARY SOURCES

ʿAbd al-Bāqī, Muḥammad Fu'ad. *Al-Muʿjam al-Mufahras li Alfāẓ al-Qur'ān al-Karīm*. Beirut: Mu'assassat Jamāl li'l-Nashr, n.d.

ʿAbd-el-Jalīl, J.-M. *Marie et l'Islam*. Paris: Beauchesne, 1950.

Abdul Razack, Ismail and Abdul Jawad al-Banna. *Women and the Family in the Sunnah of the Prophet*. International Centre for Population Studies and Research, al-Azhar. Cairo: Dār al-Kutub, n.d.

Badawī, ʿAbd al-Salām Muḥammad. *Maryam al-Batūl: Mithāl al-Umm al-Ḥanūn*. Cairo: Dār al-Anṣār, 1978.

Baljon, J.M.S., 'Prophetology of Shāh Walī Allāh,' *Islamic Studies*, 9:1 (March 1970), 69-79.

Baron, Salo Wittmayer. *A Social and Religious History of the Jews*. NY.: Columbia Univ. Press, 1950.

Barr, Martha, "ʿĪsā: The Islamic Christ,' *The Islamic Quarterly*, 33:4 (1989) 236-62.

Bū-Dhīna, Muḥammad. *Abu'l-Ḥasan al-Shādhilī*. Tunis: Dār al-Turkī li'l-Nashr, 1989.

Burckhardt, Titus (see al-Darqāwī).

Chejne, Anwar G. *Islam and the West: the Moriscos, A Cultural and Social History*. Albany: SUNY Press, 1983.

Chittick, William C. *The Sufi Path of Knowledge: Ibn al-ʿArabī's Metaphysics of Imagination*. Albany: SUNY Press, 1989.

Courtois, V. *Mary in Islam*. Calcutta: The Little Flower Press, 1954.

Cresswell, K.A.C. *A Short Account of Early Muslim Architecture*. Baltimore: Penguin Books, Inc., 1958.

al-Darqāwī, al-ʿArabī. *Letters of a Sufi Master*, trans .& notes Titus Burckhardt. London: Perennial Books, 1973.

De Bunes Ibarra, Miguel Angel. *Los Moriscos en el Pensamiento Histórico: Historiografía de un Grupo Marginado*. Madrid: Ediciones Catedra, 1983.

Diccionario de la Lengua Castellana. por la Real Academia Española. Madrid, 1914.

Encyclopedia Biblica. ed. T.K. Cheyne and J. Sutherland. London: Adam & Chas. Black, 1898–1903.

Encyclopedia of Islam (new ed.). Leiden: Brill, 1971– .

Encyclopedia Judaica. Jerusalem: Keter Publishing House Ltd., 1971 (vol. 12).

Encyclopedia of Religion and Ethics, eds., James Hastings and L. Gray. N.Y.: Scribner's and Sons, 1981.

Epalza, Miguel de, 'Un Manuscrito Narrativo Normativo Arabe y Aljamiado: Problemas Linguisticos y Teologicos de las Traducciones Moriscas,' *Les Actes de la Primière Table Ronde du C.I.E.M.*, ed. Abdeljelīl Temīmī. no. 13, Tunis, 1986, 35-45.

Epstein, Isidore, ed. *Babylonian Talmud* (English text). London: Soncino Press, 1935.

Epstein, Louis M. *Marriage Laws in the Bible and the Talmud*. Cambridge (Mass.): Harvard University Press, 1942.

García-Arenal, Mercedes. *Los Moriscos*. Madrid: Editoria Nacional, 1975.

Gayangos, Pascual de, 'Language and Literature of the Moriscos,' tr. Louis Viardot (sub-title: 'Essai sur l'Histoire des Arabes et des Mores d'Espagne'). *The British and Foreign Review*, no. 15 (1839), 63-95.

al-Ghazālī, Abū Ḥamīd Muḥammad ibn Muḥammad. *The Remembrance of Death and the Afterlife* (Book 40 of *Iḥyā' 'Ulūm al-Dīn)*, trans. and notes T.J. Winter. Cambridge: The Islamic Texts Society, 1989.

Ghunaym, Aḥmad. *Al-Mar'at mundhu al-Nash'a bayn al-Tajrīm wa'l-Takrīm*. Cairo: al-Kaylānī, 1980/1401.

Gibson, Margaret Dunlop, ed. and trans. *Apocrypha Sinaitica* (Arabic and English). London: C.J. Clay & Sons, 1896.

Graves, Robert. *The Nazarene Gospel Restored*. Garden City, N.Y.: Doubleday, 1954.

Grabar, Oleg. *The Formation of Islamic Art*. New Haven: Yale Univ. Press, 1973.

Harvey, L., 'The Literary Culture of the Moriscos, 1492–1609: A Study based on the extent manuscripts in Arabic and Aljamía,' (Unpublished thesis: Magdalen College: Oxford Univ., 1958), vol. 1, 451 pp; vol. 2, 215 pp.

Haykal, Muḥammad Ḥusayn. *Ḥayāt Muḥammad.* Cairo: Dār al-Maʿārif, 1979.

Hegyi, Ottmar. *Cinco Leyendas Y Otras Relatos Moriscos* (ms. 4953 de la Biblioteca Nacional de Madrid). Madrid: Editorial Gredos, 1981.

Hennecke, Edgar. *New Testament Apocrypha,* ed., W. Schneemelcher, and trans., R. McL. Wilson. London: Lutterworth Press, 1972.

Hitti, Philip K. *Islam and the West.* Princeton: Van Nostrand Co., 1962.

———. *History of the Arabs.* London: Macmillan & Co. Ltd., 1964 (8th ed.).

Hone, William, trans. *The Apocryphal New Testament.* London: Wm. Reeves, n.d.

Jabbūr, Jibrā'īl S. *Ibn ʿAbd Rabbihi wa ʿIqduhu.* Beirut: Dār al-Jadīda, 1979.

James, Montague Rhodes. *The Apocryphal New Testament.* Oxford: Clarendon Press, 1924.

Jewish Encyclopedia, ed., Isidore Singer, et al. N.Y.: Funk and Wagnalls, 1901–1906 (12 vols.)

Journal of the Muḥyiddīn Ibn ʿArabī Society, 4 (1985): 56–59.

Kerr, Rev. David A 'Mary, Mother of Jesus in the Islamic Tradition: A Theme for Christian Muslim Dialogue,' *Encounter.* no. 155 (May 1989), 1–17.

Lemu, Aisha B. and Fatima Heeren. *Women in Islam.* England: Derbyshire Print, 1976/1396.

Lenker, Michael Karl. 'The Importance of the Riḥla for the Islamization of Spain,' (PhD. thesis, University of Pennsylvania), 1982, 377 pp.

Littmann, Enno. 'Islamisch-arabische Heiligenlieder,' *Jahrgang,* no. 2 (Akademie der Wissenschaften und der Literatur: Wiesbaden), 99–168.

Lomax, Derek W. *The Reconquest of Spain.* London and New York: Longman, 1978.

Longás y Bartibás, Pedro. *Vida Religiosa de los Moriscos*. Madrid: Centro de Estudios e Investigaciones Cientificas, 1915.

El Mancebo de Arévolo. *Tafsíra* (sixteenth-century. ms. no. 42, collection of Miguel Asín), Instituto de Filología, Madrid.

al-Mawdūdī, Abu'l-ʿAlā. *Tafsīr Sūrat al-Kahf wa-Maryam*. Cairo: al-Mukhtār al-Islāmī, 1980/1401.

McAuliffe, Jane Dammen. 'Chosen of All Women: Mary and Fatima in Qur'ānic Exegesis,' *Islamochristiana*. vol. 7 (1981), 19–28.

Meinardus, Otto F.A. *The Holy Family in Egypt*. Cairo: A.U.C. Press, 1986.

al-Najjār, ʿAbd al-Wahhāb. *Qiṣaṣ al-Anbiyā'*. Cairo: Mu'assasat al-Ḥalabī, 1966.

Narváez, María Teresa, 'El Mancebo de Arévolo Frente a Jesus y María: Tradición y Novedad,' *La Litterature Aljamiado-Morisque: Hybridisme Linguistique et Univers Discursif*, ed., Abdeljelīl Temīmī (Les actes de la première table ronde du C.I.E.M.), Tunis: Pub. du Centre de Recherche en Bibliotheconomie et Sciences de l'Information no. 13 (1986), 109–15.

Naṣr, Seyyed Ḥossein. *Ideals and Realities of Islam*, London: Mandala Books, 1966.

Netton, Ian Richard. *Ikhwān aṣ-Ṣafā'*. Rome: Academia Nazionale dei Lincei, 1981.

———. *Allah Transcendent: Studies in the Structure and Semiotics of Islamic Philosophy, Theology and Cosmology*. London: Routledge, 1989.

New Schaff-Herzog Encyclopedia of Religious Knowledge, eds., Jackson, S.M., G.W. Gilmore, et al. Michigan: Barker Book House, 1950s.

Pano y Ruata, Mariano de. *Las Coplas del Peregrino de Puey Monçón: viaje a la Meca en el siglo* XVI, Intro. de Eduardo de Saavedra. Zaragoza, ti de Comas Hermanos, 1897.

Parrinder, Geoffrey. *Jesus in the Qur'an*. London: Sheldon Press, 1982.

Rahbar, Daud, 'The Tradition of the Qur'ānic Exegesis,' *Muslim World*, 52:4 (Oct. 1962), 296–307.

Rosenthal, Franz. *The Technique and Approach of Muslim Scholarshi* Roma: Pontificum Institutium Biblicium (Analecta Orientalia no. 24), 1947.

Rūmī, Jalāl al-Dīn. *The Mathnawi*, ed. & trans., R.A. Nicholson. Cambridge: Univ. Press, 1977 (3 vols.).

Schacht, Joseph. *The Origins of Islamic Jurisprudence.* Oxford: Clarendon Press, 1950.

Schimmel, Annemarie. *Mystical Dimensions of Islam.* Chapel Hill: University of North Carolina Press, 1975.

Schleifer, Aliah. *Motherhood in Islam.* Louisville, Ky.: Islamic Texts Society–U.S.A., 1986.

Schleifer, S. Abdullah, 'Islamic Jerusalem as Archetype of a Harmonious Environment,' *The Middle East City: Ancient Traditions Confront a Modern World*, ed., Abdulaziz Saqqaf. Paragon House, 1986.

Schneemelcher, Wilheim, ed. *New Testament Apocrypha* (rev. ed.). (Cambridge: James Clarke & Co. Ltd.) Louisville: Westminster/John Knox Press, 1991, vol. 1.

al-Shawkānī, Muḥammad ibn ʿAlī ibn Muḥammad (d. 1250 AH). *Nayl al-Awṭār*. Cairo: Maktabat al-Kulliyyāt al-Azhariyya, n.d.

Shorter Encyclopedia of Islam, ed., H.A.R. Gibb & J.H. Kramers. Leiden: Brill, 1961.

Ṣiddīqī, Muḥammad Zubayr. *Ḥadīth Literature: Its Origin, Development, Special Features and Criticism.* Calcutta University, 1961.

Smith, Jane I. and Yvonne Y. Haddad, 'The Virgin Mary in Islamic Tradition and Commentary,' *Muslim World*, 79:3-4 (July/Oct. 1989), 161-87.

Smith, Margaret. *Rābiʿa the Mystic.* California: Rainbow Bridge Co. Ltd., 1977.

Sparks, H.F.D., ed. *The Apocryphal Old Testament.* Oxford: Clarendon Press, 1984.

al-ʿUlaymi, ʿAbd al-Raḥmān ibn Muḥammad. *Kitāb al-Uns al-Jalīl bi Tarīkh al-Quds wa'l-Khalīl.* Cairo: al-Matbaʿat al-Wahbiyya, 1866/1283.

Waddy, Charis. *Women in Muslim History.* London: Longman, 1980.

Wālī Allāh, Shāh. *Ta'wīl al-Aḥādīth fī Rumūz Qiṣaṣ al-Anbiyā': A Mystical Interpretation of Prophetic Tales by an Indian Muslim*, trans., J.M.S.Baljon. Leiden: E.J.Brill, 1973.

Wehr, Hans. *A Dictionary of Modern Written Arabic*, J. Milton Cowan, ed., Wiesbaden: Otto Harrassowitz, 1979 (4th ed.).

Wensinck, A.J. *Muᶜjam al-Mufahras li-Alfāẓ al-Ḥadīth al-Nabawī*. Leiden: E.J. Brill, 1936.

al-Zirr, Maddāwī and ᶜAbdullāh Nūr al-Dīn Durkee, trans. & Notes. *School of the Shādhdhuliyyah*. Cairo: Shaykh ᶜAbd al-Ḥalīm Maḥmud Society, 1992/1412, vol. 1.

Annotated Index / Glossary

Aaron (Hārūn), 25, 36–37, 45, 70, 110, 113–14, 117, 126
ablution, 28, 56
Abraham (Ibrāhīm, 15, 22, 43,48, 57, 76, 84–86, 101–3, 106, 117, 120, 133, 137
Abū Bakr aṣ Ṣiddīq (the first Caliph of Islam; father of ʿĀ'isha), 87, 106–7, 116–19, 124-25, 129 [Also, see *ṣiddīq*]
Abū Dāwūd, 47, 59, 102–4, 121, 137
Abū Hurayra, 22, 35, 47, 49, 59, 75–76, 78, 113–14, 120, 125, 127
Abū Yaʿlā, 27, 118
Abyssinia (modern name: Ethiopia), 97, 104, 138
ʿĀd (According to Arabian tradition, an ancient people who occupied a large part of the southern Arabian peninsula), 44, 116–17
Adam (Ādam), 33, 79, 98, 111
ʿadhrā' (virgin), 66
ahl al-kitāb: The People of the Book: Jews and Christians, 22, 106
ʿĀ'isha: wife of the Prophet Muḥammad; daughter of Abū Bakr aṣ-Ṣiddīq; narrator of ḥadīths, 50, 63, 68, 70–71, 76, 80–81, 104, 124–25, 137
ʿālam al-mulk: the material world, 131
ʿālayhā as-salām: Peace be upon her (a prayer which is traditionally reserved for prophets)
ʿAlī: the fourth Caliph of Islam; the son-in-law of the Prophet Muḥammad, husband of Fāṭima; narrator of ḥadīths, 10, 26, 63, 102, 124
ʿālim (plur. *ʿulamā*): a religious scholar, 81, 124, 126, 128
Aljamía: generally used to describe the Romance language which was written in Magrebi script by the Moriscos of post-Andalusian Spain, 134–35
Allah (Allāh): the Supreme Being, 15, 51, 66, 89–90, 93, 104, 111, 117, 119, 128–33, 136
Allāhu aʿlam: Allah knows best (what the truth of the matter is), 115
Amalekite, 128
Andrew, 42
angel/angels, 27, 30–31, 38, 44, 56–57, 60, 64, 71, 77–78, 81, 83–86, 90, 92, 110–13, 115
Apocrypha/apochryphal, 114, 116
apostles of Allah: Prophets who came with a Message; Messengers of ʿĪsā [Jesus], 42–43
ʿaql: rationality, intellect, mind, 25, 89, 118, 129
aqlām: arrows; reeds used for pens, 27

Anna (Ḥanna), 22–25, 36, 55, 86, 90, 106–8
Arabia, 107, 117
Arabic, 22–23, 34, 42, 55, 65, 75, 97, 106–7, 114–16, 134–35
Aramaic, 25, 107–8
Ascension, 34, 41, 112
al-Ashʿarī, 78, 126, 128
ʿAshyā (see Elizabeth)
Āsiyā: wife of Pharaoh, 39, 64, 69, 77, 80, 128
athār (sing. *athar*): traces; accounts that have come down from the past, 114–15, 119
awliyā' (sing. *walī*), 53, 80, 82, 86–90, 111, 119, 126, 128–31
āya (plur. *āyāt*): a verse of the Qur'ān; a sign, 27, 32, 35, 70, 100, 106, 108, 110, 118, 123, 124, 128
al-Azraqī, 101–3, 105
Badawī, 24, 37, 40–41, 52–53, 61, 92, 107–12, 114–17, 119, 121, 133
balsam (balm; balsan), 40
batūl: an ephithet for Mary, a chaste, pious woman, who is distinguished from others due to her spirituality and beauty; one who has isolated herself for devotional purposes, 66, 107–12, 114–17, 119, 121, 123–24, 126–27, 133, 136–38
Bayt Laḥm (Bethlehem), 34, 38, 112
Bayt al-Maqdis (the Holy Enclosure; the Temple area of the Ḥaram ash Sharīf); it may also refer to the greater area of Jerusalem (modern name: al-Quds), 23, 25, 73, 106, 109, 112, 114
Bethlehem (see Bayt Laḥm)
Bible, 9, 107
bil maʿrūf: the best you can
bint: [the]daughter [of], 23, 43, 106, 123–24
birth, 22, 24, 27, 33–37, 54, 60, 67, 84, 90, 125, 127
al-Bukhārī, 22, 47, 49, 51, 58, 102, 104, 106, 112–13, 117–24, 126–27, 137–38
Cairo (al-Qāhira), 5, 13, 17, 19, 40, 97–98, 100, 114, 134
Canaan, 128
chaste/chastity, 31, 43, 57, 65, 67, 69–70, 96
Chejne, 134
children, 15, 17, 23, 46, 50, 75, 79, 113, 124
Christian/Christianity, 10, 16, 21, 28, 40–42, 65, 78, 97, 101, 111, 122, 134
Companions of the Prophet Muḥammad (*aṣ-ṣaḥāba*), 30, 34, 68, 71, 81, 102
conception, 23, 29–33, 35, 52, 54, 57, 60, 72, 92, 129, 134
Courtois, 9, 112
cradle, 37–38, 51, 57, 61, 90, 112
al-Daḥdāḥ (cemetery of al-Faradīs in Damascus), 43
aḍ-Ḍaḥḥāk, 30,71
Damascus, 18, 38–39, 43, 107, 115
David (the prophet Dāwūd), 22–23, 47, 59, 73, 102–4, 106, 110, 114, 121, 137
death, 5, 22, 24, 35–36, 41–42, 58–60, 68, 113, 116–17, 131
devout/devoutness, 12, 20, 61, 96
al-Dhahabī, 122
adh-dhāt: essence; ipsiety; *Adh-Dhāt*: the Essence in the absolute meaning, the Ultimate Reality, 132

dīwān: collection of poetry, 133–34
doctrine/doctrinal, 5, 50–51, 86
*du*ʿ*ā'*: voluntary supplication, 39, 61, 79, 87–88, 98–99, 129
East (*mashriq*), 29, 131
Egypt, 19, 38, 40, 51, 97, 113, 135
Elijah, 57
Elizabeth (ʿAsiyā), 32, 73, 108
Ephesus (Afsus): today called Kucuk Menderes, in west Turkey, south of Izmir, 42, 115–16
Eve (Hawwā'), 72, 92, 113
Farādīs, 43
fast/fasting, 33–35, 37, 60, 68, 96, 112, 121, 123
Fāṭima: daughter of the Prophet Muḥammad; wife of ʿAlī; mother of Ḥasan and Ḥusayn, 12, 26–27, 63–65, 71–72, 75–76, 80–81, 122–25, 133
fiṭra: an innate disposition to the Truth; primordial character, 78, 91–92, 125, 131, 135
al-Ghazālī, 99, 118, 131
Gabriel (Jibrīl), 27, 30–31, 34, 60, 64, 71, 73, 81, 85, 89, 109–12, 129–30, 136
gharīb: strange (see also ḥadīth), 39, 64
ghusl: the major ritual ablution which entails the washing of the entire body, 28, 56
God (see Allah)
Gospels, 29, 42, 115
Greek, 107
grotto, 28, 30
guardian/guardianship, 24–26, 29, 44, 55, 109
al-ḥadath: the temporal world, 132
ḥadīth/ḥadīths (Ar. plur. *aḥādīth*): saying of the Prophet Muḥammad or the Companions. Ḥadīth clasifications: *ṣaḥīḥ*: sound: *ḥasan*: good; *qawwī*: strong; *gharīb*: strange; *bāṭil*: erroneous; *matrūk/munkar*: rejected: *mawdū*ʿ: forged. (For "chain of authorities," see *isnād*), 11, 14, 18–22 ff (throughout text)
Ḥafsa: wife of the Prophet Muḥammad, 70, 125
Ḥājar (Hagar, the mother of Ishmael), 56, 120
ḥajj: the greater pilgrimage, which includes specific rites at the Holy sanctuary of Mecca and at Mount Arafat, which is believed to be the place where Adam and Eve reunited after the expulsion from Paradise, the symbolic stoning of Iblīs, and concludes with the Feast of the Sacrifice, a reminder of Abraham's intended sacrifice of his son. 97, 134
ḥakīm (sage; wise man), 89–90, 129
al Ḥākim, 48, 79, 122, 125
Ḥanna (see Anna, the mother of Maryam)
al-ḥaqīqa: the Reality, 92
al-ḥaqq: the Real, 130, 132
ḥalāl: allowed, 65
ḥarām: forbidden, 65, 105, 124
Ḥaram ash-Sharīf: the Holy sanctuary of Mecca or of Medina or of Jerusalem, 61
Hārūn (see Aaron)

Hārūt and Mārūt: figuratively, angelic beings; good men; the Marut of ancient Babylon (Qur'ān 2:102), 42, 115
Ḥasan: grandson of the Prophet Muḥammad, son of ʿAlī and Fāṭima, 27
al-Ḥasan al-Baṣrī, 17–20, 22, 24, 26–28, 30, 33–36, 39–42, 47–49, 51, 56, 58–65, 67–73, 75–77, 79–82, 85–86, 88, 90–92, 99–100, 102, 104, 106–34, 136–38
Hawwā' (see Eve)
heaven, 12, 52, 109
Hebrew, 22, 107–8, 110
Herod, 22, 38, 40, 42, 52, 98, 114
hijra: emigration, 136. The first *hijra* of the Muslims from Mecca to Abyssinia (AD 615). The second *hijra* of the Muslims from Mecca to Abyssinia (*c.* 615-616). The *hijra* of the Prophet to Medina (AD 623), which marks the beginning of the Muslim calender=AH or *Heg.* or H. or *h.* 136
himma: ardent effort; extreme longing for Allah, spiritual will, 91, 131, 135
Ḥūd (the Apostle sent to the ʿĀd people), 133
Ḥusayn: grandson of the Prophet Muḥammad, son of ʿAlī and Fāṭima, 27,
Iblīs: the chief devil of the jinns, 113, 127
Ibn ʿAbbās, 18–19, 23, 30, 33, 35, 39, 64, 102, 111, 122
Ibn ʿAbd Rabbihi, 111–12
Ibn ʿArabī, 60, 90–91, 99, 110, 114, 119, 121, 129–33, 135–36
Ibn al-ʿĀṣ, ʿAbdullāh ibn ʿAmr, 34, 47, 49, 71, 101, 107, 118, 129, 132
Ibn al-ʿĀṣ, ʿAmr, 34, 47, 49, 71, 101, 107, 118, 129, 132
Ibn ʿAsākir, 18, 34, 43, 64–65, 111, 116, 122
Ibn Baṭṭūṭa, 116
Ibn Fūrak, 87, 129
Ibn Ḥajar al-ʿAsqalānī, 19, 47, 58, 76, 82, 102, 106–7, 112–13, 117–24, 126–28, 134, 137–38
Ibn Ḥanbal, Aḥmad, 18–19, 47, 59, 68, 79, 104, 121, 124, 127, 134, 137
Ibn Ḥazm, 82–85, 128–29
Ibn Hishām, 19, 28, 106, 109, 115, 117
Ibn Isḥāq, 23, 28–29, 42, 106, 108, 110, 115, 126
Ibn Jarīr, 30, 108, 112–13
Ibn Kathīr, 19, 34, 39, 51, 56, 63–65, 76–77, 80–81, 106–14, 117, 119–23, 126–28, 134
Ibn Khuzayma, 79
Ibn Māja, 48
Ibn Manẓūr, 123, 125, 127
Ibn Masʿūd, 30, 67, 104
Ibn Qayyim al-Jawziyya (Ibn al-Qayyim), 29, 69–70, 110, 124–25
Ibn Qutayba, 108, 110, 112-13
Ibn Saʿd, 19, 34, 63, 106, 137
Ibrāhīm (see Abraham)
ʿidda: the waiting period for a woman before remarriage, 123
idols, 101, 127
Idrīs (a Prophet, whom some scholars have identified with the Biblical Enoch), 81, 126
ijmāʿ = *jamāʿa*: the consensus of the scholars, 47, 74

Ikhwān aṣ-Ṣafā' (the Brothers of Purity), 119
imagination (*tawahhum*), 83
Imām: Caliph; scholarly religious authority; leader of communal prayer, 87, 98, 118
ʿImrān (Joachim, the father of Mary); also, the family of ʿImrān, 22–24, 31, 36, 43, 53, 56, 63–64, 69, 75, 79, 99, 106
inspiration, arising from instinct (*ilhām*), 5, 12, 30, 83, 86, 100, 112; divine inspiration (*waḥyī*), 30
intercession, 104–5
ʿĪsā ibn Maryam (the prophet Jesus), 27, 101–2, 111
Isaac (the prophet Isḥāq), 15, 22, 43, 58, 84, 102, 117, 126
Isaiah, 113
al-Isfarā'inī, 129
Isḥāq (see Isaac)
Ishmael (the prophet Ismāʿīl), 15, 22, 43, 58, 102, 117, 126!
Ismāʿīl (see Ishmael)
isnād (chain of authorities), 30, 64, 103, 117, 122
al-Isrā' wa al-Miʿrāj: the miraculous night journey (*al-isrā'*) of the Prophet Muḥammad and his ascension (*al-miʿrāj*) from Jerusalem to the seven heavens on the 27th of the Islamic month, Rajab), 112
Israel (Isrā'īl), 15, 21, 35, 39, 65, 105, 108, 112–13, 116
Isrā'īl (see Israel)
Isrā'īlī sources (Isrā'īliyyāt): a technical term referring to data which traditional Muslim Scholars identify as originating from Christian or Jewish sources, 21, 65, 116
iʿtikāf: the World of Sovereignty or the Prescence of the Secrets, 68, 123–24
Jacob (the prophet Yaʿqūb), 15, 22, 43, 84, 106
jadhb: attraction, 130
majdhūb: one whom Allah chooses for the divine attraction to Him, 91
Jaʿfar, 49
al-janna: Paradise, 127
Jerusalem (Bayt al-Maqdis; the city of al-Quds), 13, 23, 29, 31, 33–34, 38, 40, 43, 61, 64, 66, 106–7, 110, 112–13, 123, 126
Jesus (ʿĪsā ibn Maryam), 5, 9–10, 13, 15, 22, 28, 33–46, 51–53, 57, 60, 79–80, 86, 90, 92–95, 97, 100-101, 103, 105, 108, 11–12, 115, 117, 125, 127, 129, 133, 137
Jewish/Jews, 78
Jibrīl (see Gabriel)
jihād: the greater *jihād*: to struggle with the soul/ego the lesser *jihād*: to struggle against non-believers, 47–48, 117–18
jinn, 63, 83
Joachim (see ʿImrān, the father of Mary)
John (the prophet Yaḥyā), 27, 32, 35–36, 42, 90, 108–9, 111, 115–16, 130
Joseph (Yūsuf, the prophet) 60, 85, 109, 111–12, 114–16, 125
Joseph (Yūsuf, the husband of Mary), 28–33, 37–38, 40–41, 66, 125–26, 136
Judea, 114
Juyūshī Mosque, 100, 136

Kaʿbā: a cubical structure in the Holy Sanctuary of Mecca, which fixes the direction of prayer for all Muslims. According to Islam, The original Kaʿbā was constructed by the prophet Abraham and his son, the prophet Ishmael. It remained a holy sanctuary and a site of pilgrimage for the monotheistic descendants of Ishmael until the Banu Khuzāʿa took custody of it and introduced idol worship. At the time of the birth of the Prophet Muḥammad, it was a place of pilgrimage for a variety of worshippers, including some Christians. When the Muslims finally captured Mecca, the idols were destroyed, and it became once again a site for monotheistic worship and pilgrimage, 19, 35, 65, 111

kahāna: predicting; fortune-telling, 83

kamāl (vb. *kamula*): perfection; completeness, 81–82, 85, 91, 107

karāma (plur. *karāmāt*): miracle(s) for saints (*awliyā*), 86–87, 89

Khadīja: the first wife of the Prophet Muḥammad and the nother of all his surviving children, 12, 63–65, 71–72, 75–76, 80–81, 122, 125, 128

al-Khalīl: an epithet for Abraham; the beloved friend of Allah, 137

al-Khāzin, 66

Kitāb: Book, 40, 106

Koran (see Qur'ān)

kuffār (sing. *kāfir*): non-believers, 48, 118; *kufr*: disbelief, 48, 62, 118

Lot (the prophet Lūṭ), 69–70, 108

mā' zamzam: the water of Zamzam in the Holy Sanctuary of Mecca, which, according to Islam, this spring arose in answer to Hagar's prayer, 58, 101, 120

al-Madīna: (Medina; Yathrib): the capital city of Islam under the first Caliphs; the first mosque is there; the Prophet and many companions are buried there; it is customary to visit Medina and Jerusalem before or after the greater or the lesser pilgrimage, 124, 136

Madyan (Midian)/ Midianites: the Midianites were nomadic Arabs, probably intermarried with the Canaanites; in the time of Moses, their territory was north-east Sinai, 114

Maghribī: pertaining to the Magreb, i.e., North Africa, 134

majdhūb (see *jadhb*)

Makka/Makkan (Mecca; Bakka); the most sacred city in Islam; it encompasses the Kaʿba and other sites holy to Muslims, and is therefore known as *umm al-qurā* (the Mother of Towns); a commercial centre and a pilgrimage site dominated by the Quraysh at the time of the birth of Muḥammad, 19, 97, 101–3, 120, 134

al-malakūt: the Kingdom, 131

ʿālam al-malakūt: the World of the Attributes, 131

Mālik/Mālikī, 71, 125, 134
Mancebo de Arévalo, 99
al-Maqdisī, 23, 25, 73, 106, 109, 112, 114
al-Maqrīzī, 40
Maram (Aramaic for Mary), 107,
ma'rifa: spiritual knowledge; gnosis, 60
marriage, 44, 66–67, 69, 110, 124
martyr (*shahīd*), 82
Mārūt (see Hārūt)
al-mashriq (the East); the metaphysical orientation of the spirit to a higher plane, 131
Maṭariyya, 98
Mecca (see Makka)
Medina see (al-Madīna)
Messenger (*rasūl*), 15, 22, 26–27, 31, 35, 37, 39, 41, 44, 47–48, 53, 58–59, 63–64, 67–68, 70–71, 73–75, 78–79, 84, 86, 89, 92–94, 101–4, 126, 128, 133
Messiah (see also 'Īsā ibn Maryam), 9-10, 15–16, 28, 34, 41, 93
Middle Ages, 42
miḥrāb: a prayer sanctuary; a prayer niche, 24, 26–30, 36, 56, 61, 73, 85, 90, 99–100, 106, 108, 110, 136
Mir, 40, 118
miracle(s) (see *mu'jiza*; *karāma*), 12, 27, 33, 87–88, 97, 129
Mi'rāj (See Isrā')
Miriam (Heb. for Mary), 107, 113
Morisco(s): the secret Muslims who remained in Spain after the fall of Granada, having been nominally baptized, 97, 99, 134
Moses (the prohet Mūsā), 11, 15, 22, 28, 37, 43, 64, 70, 76–77, 79–80, 84, 86, 106, 109, 113–15, 117, 122, 126, 128, 133
Mount of Olives (*jabal az-zaytūn*), 28, 43
mubāḥ (permissable), 105
Muḥammad, born in Mecca in 570, of Qurayshi origin; the Seal of the Prophets, according to Islam; among his titles are: Aḥmad (the Most Commendable) and Muṣṭafā (the Chosen One), 8, 15, 20, 22, 24, 71, 77, 79, 81, 85, 95, 98, 112, 116, 120, 123, 125–26, 129, 131, 133
Mujāhid, 19, 30, 39, 56, 62, 112, 121,
al-Muḥāsibī, 47
mu'jiza (plur. *mu'jizāt*): miracle(s) for prophets, 87, 89
Muqātil, 19, 33, 62, 106, 109–10, 115, 121
murakkab: acceptance of Allah's Will to go wherever His Will carries one, 135
murāqaba: the constate state of spiritual vigilance, 91, 130, 136
Mūsā (see Moses)
Muslim: one who has surrendered to the Will of Allah; one who has accepted Islam as his/her religion; Moslem
muṣṭafā: the chosen/selected, 70, 125
mystic/mystical/mysticism, 53
nabī (prophet)/*nabiyya* (prophetess), 74, 86, 94, 133
nafs: soul/ego, 72, 117–18, 130
Najrān (located in northern Yemen; Negrana), 37, 114
al-Nasā'ī, 34, 47–48, 58, 104

Naṣāra (Nazareth), 28, 34, 37, 49, 54, 70, 78–80, 83, 91, 106, 109, 115, 117–20, 123–24, 126–27, 129, 133–38
Nazarene, 34, 110
Nicodemus, 42, 116
niyya: intention: The Muslim must state his intention first before undertaking obligatory acts, such as, the five daily prayers, fasting each day of the month of Ramaḍān, embarking on the pilgrimage, etc., 43, 123–24
Noah (the prophet Nūḥ), 15, 69–70, 117
nubuuwa: prophethood; prophecy, 78, 81, 83, 85
Nūḥ (see Noah)
Palestine, 19, 38, 41, 107, 115
palm, 33–34, 64, 66, 89–90, 98–99
Paradise (*al-janna*), 22, 43, 47–48, 50, 53–54, 63–65, 77, 96
parents, 5, 17, 22, 46–48, 51, 78, 117–18
Parrinder, 9, 101, 137
Pharaoh, 64, 69, 77, 80, 128
poetry, 43, 97, 133
Pontius Pilate, 42
prayer (see *du*ʿ*ā'*), 79, 87
 prayer (see *ṣalāt*)
 prayers (*sunna*): voluntary, but formal,. prayers, according to the practice of the Prophet Muḥammad, for example, the additional prayers before and/or after each of the five daily prayers or upon entering a mosque
prophecy (*nubuuwa*), 76, 78, 81–87
prophet/ prophetess (*nabī*/ *nabiyya*) 12, 15, 18–19, 21 ff.
prophethood (*nubuuwa*), , 74–76, 78, 80–83, 87–88, 93, 126
prostration (*sajda*), 56–57, 61
puberty, 24, 27–28, 56
pure/purity, 28, 30–32, 37, 43, 54, 57, 62, 65–67, 69, 72, 77, 79, 90, 92, 95–96, 99
qāḍī: a judge whose decisions are based on Islamic Law, 19, 105, 138
al-Qahira (see Cairo)
Qatāda, 20, 25, 30, 112, 115, 127
qibla: the direction to which Muslims turn in prayer.
 the first *qibla*: Jerusalem
 the second and present *qibla*: the Kaʿba in Mecca, 100, 136
qidam: Eternity, 132
qiṣṣa (plur. *qiṣaṣ*: story; legend (used as a technical designation, in contrast to ḥadīth), 29–30, 34, 41, 52, 97–98, 102, 113,115
al-Quds (Jerusalem), 40
al-qunūt: submissiveness, devoutness, obedience to Allah; steadfastness in prayer
 al-qānitūn: those possessing these characteristics, 56
Qur'ān (Koran): the Holy Scripture revealed to Muḥammad via the angel Gabriel, considered the authentic Word of Allah by Muslims, 9, 11, 15–16, 18–24, 26, 28–29, 31, 33, 35, 37–39, 41, 46, 51–52, 54–55, 57–58, 62, 65, 67, 71–72, 74, 81, 83, 85, 92–93, 95–96, 100, 106, 115–17, 120, 122, 125–28, 130, 133–34, 136

Quraysh: the Arabian tribe of the Prophet Muḥammad, 126
al-Qurṭubī, 23, 43, 120
Qūsiya, 40
rabwa: hill, 38–39
raḍiya/Allāhu ʿanhā: May Allah be pleased with her
rakaʿa/rukūʿ: bowing, kneeling in prayer, 56
Ramaḍān: the ninth month of the Islamic calendar. It is incumbent upon all Muslims, who are physically able to do so, during this month to fast every day from all food and liquid intake and from undesirable speech—from the time of the call to the dawn prayer to the call of the sunset prayer, 68, 107, 123–24
Ramla, 38-39, 114
rasūl: messenger, 94, 133
revelation, 12, 19, 71, 78, 81, 83–84, 86, 92–93, 100, 125
riḥla: in Andalusia, it was a technical term denoting specifically a trip with the intent to undertake religious studies abroad, 134
Rosenthal, 128
rukkāb: the person who fully accepts Allah's Will over his/her destiny (see *murakkab*), 131
Rūm (the ancient Roman Empire), 69–70, 110, 124, 137–38
rumūz (sin. *ramz*): signs, indications, 90
ru'yā: a vision that results from Divine revelation, 83–84
Rūzbihān al-Baqlī, 20, 60–61, 72, 91–92, 121, 125–26, 130, 132, 136
ṣaḥīḥ (see ḥadīth), 21,64, 85, 125
saint (*walī/waliyya*), 10–11, 20, 82, 86, 89, 126, 129
sajda: prostation in prayer, 56, 61
ṣalāt: ritual prayer. The five ritual prayers in Islam are the dawn prayer (*ṣalāt al-fajr*), the midday prayer (*ṣalāt al-ẓuhr*), the afternoon prayer (*ṣalāt al-ʿaṣr)*, the sunset prayer (*ṣalāt al-maghrib*), and the evening prayer (*ṣalāt al-ʿishā'*).
Ṣāliḥ (Arab Prophet), 114, 133
Ṣalla Allāhu ʿalayhi wa sallam: May the Peace and Blessings of Allah be upon him (a prayer said for the Prophet Muḥammad)
sanctuary (*miḥrāb*), 24, 26, 61, 64, 73, 99–100, 120
Sāra (Sarah), 28,57, 70, 84, 106, 109, 115, 117, 120, 134, 137
Satan (*ash-Shaytān*), 24, 78–79, 88, 109, 117, 127, 135
sayyida: lady, mistress; (with reference to Mary): the chief lady, mistress, 27, 63
al-Shādh(dh)ulī (frequently called al-Shādhulī or al-Shadhlī) is the title bestowed upon the Sufi shaykh, ʿAlī Abū al-Ḥasan, born in 1196/593 in Morocco. He received this title in a visionary dream (*ru'ya*) in which he heard His Lord say to him: "O ʿAlī! You are ash-Shādhu lī . . . meaning: I have set you apart for Me." The title is not related to the name of the village of Shādhila in Tunis.

al-Shahāda: the statement, testimonial; the basis of the Muslim creed: "I bear witness that there is no god, except Allah and I bear witness that Muḥammad is the messenger of Allah," 131
shahīd (fem. *shahīda*; plur. *shuhadā'*): martyr(s), 82
al-Shām (previously, the northern part of the ancient Arabian peninsula; currently, Syria or its capital city, Damascus), 41
sharīʿā: Islamic Law based on the Qur'ān and the Sunna of the Prophet Muḥammad, and its early codification. In Sunni Islam, the Four Schools of Law are: Mālikī, Shāfiʿī, Ḥanafī, and Ḥanbalī, 107, 123, 138
shaykh: a master of the traditional religious subjects; a spiritual guide for seekers of the Truth, 130, 132
shirk: Polytheism; attributing Allah's powers to anything other than Allah, 105
shuhūd (*mushāhada*): witnessing; a synonym for unveiling; opening to the Unseen Worlds, 132
ṣidq: truth, sincerity, correctness, 125
ṣiddīq (*ṣiddīqa*); righteous, trustworthy, truthful, sincere of faith and belief, 43, 60, 70, 73–74, 78, 81–82, 85, 93–94, 125
sign, 10, 16, 26, 31, 38, 43–44, 46, 51, 54, 68, 72, 81, 93–94, 96, 99
Silwān, 66
Simon Peter, 42
sīra: biography of the Prohet Muḥammad, 28, 70, 106, 109, 115, 117, 120, 134, 137
sirr: secret; secret heart, inner consciousness, 90, 129
Spain/Spanish, 17–18, 20, 23, 97, 99, 128, 134–35
Spirit (*ar-rūḥ*), 5, 13, 29–31, 69, 92–93, 99, 110–11, 130–31, 133
spirituality, 54, 65, 91–92, 96, 99, 123
submission, 43, 53–57, 60–61, 79, 89, 94, 96, 100, 105, 133
Sufi/Sufism: Islamic mystic/mysticism, 20, 25, 47, 60, 86, 112, 118, 130–32, 136
Sulaymān (the prophet Solomon), 23
Sunna (plur. *sunan*): usually refers to the deeds, utterances and unspoken approval of the Prophet Muḥammad or also to that of the first four Caliphs. And in Islamic jurisprudence (*fiqh*), the word sunna = recommended, 67–68, 100, 102, 120–22, 137
Sunni, 15, 21–22, 24, 33, 42, 47, 74, 86, 95–96, 100, 105, 133
sūra: a chapter in the Qur'ān; sura, 28, 70, 106, 109, 115, 117, 120, 134, 137
sustenance, 24, 26–27, 35, 54, 89, 100, 109
symbol, 13, 43, 51, 61, 69, 89, 94, 100
Syriac, 42, 107–8
al-Ṭabarī, 23, 48–49
tafsīr (plur. *tafāsīr*): explication of the Qur'ān; also, see: *mufassirūn*, 106–14, 117, 119–23, 125–30

Talmud/Talmudic, 57, 110, 113, 119–20
ta'wīl: explanation of the underlying meanings of Qur'ānic passages, 110, 128–30
Temple (Bayt al-Maqdis), 23–25, 28–30, 32, 37–38, 61, 86, 106, 109, 111
al-Thaʿlabī, 111
Thamūd (An ancient people, probably of eastern and central Asia in the area of Petra prior to the Nabateans), 114–16
tharīd: a dish consisting of thin Arab bread soaked in a vegetable or meat stew, 80, 127
al-Tirmidhī, 47, 51, 122
token (see also sign), 31
Torah, 15, 22, 93, 108
Turkey, 115
ʿulamā' (see *ʿālim*)
Umayya, 116
umma: the greater community of Muslims; contemporarily, sometimes used to designate a particular national community of Muslims, 35, 43, 63, 71, 75, 80, 105, 133
ʿUthmān (the third Caliph of Islam), 68
al-ʿUmar ibn al-Khaṭṭāb (the second Caliph of Islam), 64, 103, 138
al-ʿUzā'ī, 56, 125
Virgin (*al-ʿadhrā'*), 5–6, 9–12, 15–16, 18, 29, 31, 34, 52, 57, 59–61, 65–66, 68, 71, 96, 98, 108, 115, 123, 132 also, see *batūl*
walī (fem. *waliyya*; plur. *awliyā'*): the beloved (by Allah), the friend (of Allah), the victorious (for Allah); a saintly, holy man or woman, 53, 74, 80, 82, 86–90, 93, 111, 119, 126, 128–31
wilāya: the state of being a saint, 129
al-Wāqidī, 103
wijā: container used by women for the cleansing of blood, 123
witnessing (*shuhūd*), 90–92, 132
women, 5–6, 11-13, 43, 49, 53, 62–72, 74–83, 85–86, 89, 92, 94–96, 99, 115, 118, 122–24, 128, 133, 136
Yaʿqūb (see Jacob)
Yāqūt, 34, 39, 111-12, 114-15
Yūsuf (see Joseph the prophet and Joseph the carpenter)
Zachariah (the prophet Zakariyyā), 24–32, 35–36, 55–57, 91–93, 97, 99–100, 108–0, 113, 135
Zakariyyā (see Zachariah)
al-Zamakhsharī, 37
al-Zajjāj, 62

MARY ✠ THE BLESSED VIRGIN OF ISLAM • Aliah Schleifer

$15.95 • ISLAMIC SPIRITUALITY / WOMEN'S STUDIES • ISBN 1-887752-02-

An in-depth study of the traditional scholarship examining the life and char-acteristics of Mary from the perspective of Sunni Islam in the classical peri-od, which took place over centuries in regions stretching from Central Asia tc Spain. Dr. Aliah Schleifer was a specialist in Islamic Studies and a professoi at the American University in Cairo; she is also the author of *Motherhood ir Islam*. The present study contains a foreword by **Timothy Winter** of Cam-bridge University's faculty of Divinity and an introduction by **Dr. Ali Jum'a Muḥammad**, Professor of Law at Al-Azhar University in Cairo.

"Christians often find it curious that Mary figures so prominently in the Qur'an and in Muslim spiritual life. She is seen as the faithful servant o the Lord who allows God's Word to bring Jesus to life in her miraculously and so give the world a prophet whom Muslims revere. This work shows ir inspiring detail the manner in which Muslim life and practice bring Mary to life as a faithful servant of the one God."

— David Burrell, C.S.C.
Hesburgh Prof. of Philosophy and Theology, Univ. of Notre Dame

"As a Catholic priest it quite surprised me to find that it was the sacrec words found in the Qur'an of Islam that provided me with what I wa yearning to know about the Blessed Mary. As one who seeks to understanc her role better, I found the Qur'an brought home to me the gifts of this amazing creature. It is very beautiful to know that when any Muslim men-tions Mary, he or she always refers to her as, 'Our Lady Mary — May the peace of God be on her.' In this important book, Mary has been describec as possessing 'the perfection of human spiritual attainment' and as being 'amongst the first group of prophets to enter Paradise.' The book empha-sizes that she is a 'spiritual example for mankind.'"

— Father Vernon Robertson
The Oratory of Our Lady and Saint Phillip, Louisville, Kentucky

FONS VITAE

ISBN 188775202-1

9 781887 752022